Aging Is Living

MYTH-BREAKING STORIES FROM LONG-TERM CARE

By Irene Borins Ash & Irv Ash

Photos by Irene Borins Ash in collaboration with Dr. Irvin Rubincam

DUNDURN PRESS

TORONTO

Editor: Michael Carroll
Copy Editor: Andrea Waters
Design: Jennifer Scott
Printer: Marquis

Library and Archives Canada Cataloguing in Publication

Borins Ash, Irene, 1952-
    Aging is living : myth-breaking stories from long-term care / by Irene Borins Ash and Irv Ash.

ISBN 978-1-55002-883-6

    1. Nursing home patients--Canada--Biography. 2. Long-term care facilities--Canada.
3. Older people--Canada--Biography. 4. Older people--Institutional care--Canada. I. Ash,
Irv II. Title.

HV1454.B67 2009   362.16092'271   C2008-908045-9

1   2   3   4   5   13   12   11   10   09

Conseil des Arts
du Canada

Canada Council
for the Arts

ONTARIO ARTS COUNCIL
CONSEIL DES ARTS DE L'ONTARIO

Canadä

We acknowledge the support of the **Canada Council for the Arts** and the **Ontario Arts Council** for our publishing program. We also acknowledge the financial support of the **Government of Canada** through the **Book Publishing Industry Development Program** and **The Association for the Export of Canadian Books**, and the **Government of Ontario** through the **Ontario Book Publishers Tax Credit program**, and the **Ontario Media Development Corporation**.

Care has been taken to trace the ownership of copyright material used in this book. The author and the publisher welcome any information enabling them to rectify any references or credits in subsequent editions.

J. Kirk Howard, President

Printed and bound in Canada.
www.dundurn.com

Dundurn Press	Gazelle Book Services Limited	Dundurn Press
3 Church Street, Suite 500	White Cross Mills	2250 Military Road
Toronto, Ontario, Canada	High Town, Lancaster, England	Tonawanda, NY
M5E 1M2	LA1 4XS	U.S.A. 14150

THIS BOOK IS DEDICATED TO the late Ann Seaton, who was the source of inspiration for this book; to my eighty-five-year-young mother, Beverley Borins, who is a positive role model for so many people; and to my nieces, Adryan Bergstrom Borins and Haley Bergstrom Borins, and my nephews, Alexander Borins and Nathaniel Borins, in the hope that they will be inspired by their elders as we have been inspired by them. We have much to learn from each other.

THIS BOOK IS ALSO DEDICATED TO the late Nellie Ash and Stan Ash, Irv's mother and brother, who are in his thoughts and the thoughts of others.

Contents

Part II: Articles and Tools

Acknowledgements

There are several people I would like to thank for helping make this book a reality.

I would like to thank the Ontario Long Term Care Association and specifically Past President Bill Dillane and Director of Communications and Public Affairs Gilbert Heffern. They believed in my passion for a new view of aging and helped open the doors and access the support that allowed me to channel my passion into an exhibit and now this book. This journey would not have been possible without the sponsorship support for both the exhibit and the book provided by Christie Gardens Apartments & Care Inc., Extendicare Inc., Leisureworld Caregiving Centres, PointClickCare, Responsive Health Management, and Revera.

I would like to thank Dr. Irvin Rubincam, who collaborated with me in the photography, and Ming Fu of Bayview Photo, who helped with developing, enlarging, and mounting the images. I would like to thank several people who wrote pieces for the book and who gave an enormous amount of encouragement and support over the years: Patricia Moffat, Debby Vigoda, Ed Clements, Harry Lynch, Celia McDougal, and Lois Dent, who is the current president of and a board member of Concerned Friends.

I would also like to thank Barry Penhale and Jane Gibson, the former owners of Natural Heritage Books. When Natural Heritage Books merged with the Dundurn Group, Barry and Jane introduced me to Kirk Howard, president and publisher of The Dundurn Group.

In addition, thanks to Councillor Joe Mihevic, who believed in my project/passion from the very beginning.

I would further like to thank Etta Ginsberg McEwan, who has been one of several mentors; Anne Rubenstein, who helped with editing; Olga Hewett, who built Irene's website; Gadi Hoz, who took the photo of Irene for her website; Sandra Kerr, Mena Caravetta, and Barbara

Wright from the G. Raymond Chang School of Continuing Education at Ryerson University; Dave Cormack, who created a video of some of the seniors in the book; and Margie Wolfe, who produced my first book, *Treasured Legacies: Older & Still Great* (Second Story Press, 2003).

I sincerely appreciate the time that the lieutenant governor of Ontario, the Honourable David C. Onley, took from his busy schedule to write his appreciation for this work in the foreword.

Finally, I would like to thank all of the seniors who allowed me to interview and photograph them. They are our heroes. In addition, I would like to thank their families and the long-term care administrators of each of their homes for their assistance.

Preface

I FEEL A SENSE of awe, respect, and gratitude for the wisdom that was shared with me by the twenty-four people I interviewed for this book. The twenty-fifth person included here was a lovely woman who passed away shortly before I began the interviewing, but her legacy and the thoughts of her daughter, son, and granddaughter were shared with me.

I feel a sense of hope for myself and others because aging well despite life's numerous difficulties is not an easy task, but that is exactly what these men and women have done. Despite wars, starvation, illnesses, and the loss of children and loved ones, these remarkable men and women continue to be creative, whether it is through painting, woodcarving, leading committees, writing their memoirs, gardening, or perhaps through learning to forgive others for things that happened to them in their lifetimes.

These people will leave a legacy, a gift to others. They had the courage and sense of adventure to enter into this project and to allow me to share some of their inmost thoughts.

Foreword

BY THE HONOURABLE DAVID C. ONLEY,
LIEUTENANT GOVERNOR OF ONTARIO

At a time when baby boomers are reaching traditional retirement ages, we are seeing unprecedented examples of people living vibrant and active lives that defy the stereotypes of days gone by. However, the fact is that many who reached their retirement years long ago and who happen to reside in long-term care (LTC) facilities are continuing to live dynamic and vigorous lives.

Irene Borins Ash, in her previous work *Treasured Legacies: Older & Still Great*, combined her skills as a social worker and her gifts as a photographer to focus on positive aging despite the vicissitudes of life. She told the stories and showed the lined faces of Canada's seniors. Some, like Jean Vanier, David Suzuki, and the late June Callwood, were household names, while others were known and loved only in their own households. To this admittedly biased eye, her subjects, whether famous or everyday Canadians, had in common the serene beauty of lives well lived and enjoyed.

In this book, Ms. Borins Ash goes against mainstream media portrayals of long-term care facilities as warehouses for seniors and people with disabilities, with her descriptions and photographs of LTC residents who are enjoying active, creative, and satisfying lives. As I know from the experience of having a parent in long-term care, these are not isolated examples of a very special few. Every year the Ontario Senior Achievement Awards are presented to individuals who have chosen not to rest on the well-earned laurels of retirement, instead devoting the years after sixty-five to a wide-ranging variety of passions, good causes, and community activism. Many of the annual honourees who are chosen from a lengthy list of nominations live in long-term care. Because the everyday minutiae that can occupy so much of a senior's day are taken care of, they have more time than they have ever had to commit to fulfilling long-held dreams and ambitions.

As a lifelong champion of disability issues, I am delighted that Irene Borins Ash has turned her discerning eye and camera lens to the positive aspects of living in long-term care. She has done a great service, not just to her subjects, whose lives and achievements deserve public recognition, but also to those who, whether considering or forced by circumstances to choose long-term care, wish to address the negative images of aging in a nursing home.

Foreword

BY DR. IRVIN RUBINCAM

Irene asked if I would assist her in taking photographs for this project. Before joining the project, I shared with many of you a negative opinion of institutional care for the elderly. In my own family, we celebrated a decade of heroic effort by a husband to keep a wife from the "indignities" of a nursing home. I now know this view is too simplistic. Indeed, there is sorrow associated with the decline of mental and physical abilities, but there is another side as well, one that needs to be better understood. Life in an institutional setting can be rich and rewarding.

In these pages you will become acquainted with some remarkable men and women. I wish you could have met them in person, as Irene and I have. In their presence you soon sense that these individuals have the ability to create something positive out of changing and challenging circumstances.

Irene and I have our own challenges: how to share with you through words and pictures alone what we came to know of each of them. On a number of the photographs, we collaborated to try to convey, as best we could, the person's story. The photographs try to tell a story about the subjects by showing them in their living and working spaces. Consider the artist Irene Greenbloom. In the photograph you see her seated with a paintbrush in hand, surrounded by vibrant and beautiful paintings, continuing to pursue her artistic passion although she is blind in one eye and ninety-three years old (at the time the picture was taken). When you read the text and look at the photograph a second time, it takes on added meaning. There is no hint of the horrors of Auschwitz and the loss of her first husband, her child, and her extended family. In spite of this, Irene's world is a good place, and with each new painting it becomes a bit better.

I have been enriched by those you will meet in this book, and I hope you will have a similar experience.

Introduction

LISTENING TO THEIR VOICES

This book focuses on various residents in long-term care facilities, especially the positive facets of their lives and their thoughts and feelings. It grew from the photography and text exhibit "Aging is Living: A New Perspective," April 30, 2008. The usual item that reaches the media about long-term care homes (often called nursing homes) is the unfortunate events that sometimes occur. Most people are afraid of long-term care homes because they represent the last phase in one's life. But sometimes people have years from the time they enter the home. This book shows how to make the best of the situation by living a fulfilling life and leaving a positive legacy for family and friends.

While researching and writing this book, I found myself being challenged by family and friends who focused on the negatives; however, there is a very real positive side to life in a long-term care home that needs to be presented to the public. Having worked in long-term care homes, a retirement home, and a home support agency, as well as being a social worker and a photographer, I was a logical person to tackle this difficult topic.

The beginning of my exploration actually began more than twenty years ago. My experience working with seniors as a social worker began in 1987, when I was hired by York Community Services. Julie Bertrand and I trained and educated respite workers for a respite program that was operated jointly with York West Meals on Wheels and St. Clair West Services for Seniors. The respite workers cared for elderly or handicapped people while their caregivers had a break from their responsibilities so that they could take care of their own needs for a while.

After the program ended, I took a locum position at the Providence Healthcare Centre, which is a long-term care facility. As well as my regular social work responsibilities, such as leading pre-admission tours, providing adjustment counselling, and participating in resident care planning as a member of a multidisciplinary team, I organized and led a therapeutic music group (which I will discuss later in the Music and Dementia section). Working with this group helped develop my thinking regarding dealing with seniors and had a tremendous impact on my personal and professional growth.

When the locum position at Providence Centre was over, I did two locum positions at the Baycrest Centre for Geriatric Care. One was in the Psychiatric Day Hospital and the other was at the Terrace, which is a retirement residence. I recall that the winter I spent at the Terrace was extremely cold, bitter, and long. I was a single woman at the time and decided to fill the void by researching what the concept of spirituality was all about.

I asked Dr. Norman Berlat, a rabbi, if he would present a paper with me in the spring at Grand Rounds, a continuing education seminar put on by Baycrest that is supported by various grants. In April 1994, we did a presentation entitled "Spirituality: The Breath of Faith." Researching the topic certainly helped lift my spirits in that cold winter. The rabbi discussed religion, and I spoke about spirituality. The research had a substantial impact on the evolution of my thoughts about working with and connecting to seniors.

After working in long-term care facilities, I took a permanent position in a community-based agency. When I was case manager at St. Clair West Services for Seniors, I visited hundreds of seniors and their families in their homes over the years; the mandate was to help people remain living on their own until the task became too difficult for them and their caregivers (if they had

one), and then we would work together to find a suitable long-term care facility.

By working at Baycrest, Providence, and St. Clair West Services for Seniors, I developed an understanding of the different ways of connecting to a person through counselling, spirituality, and music, and at the same time I came to understand the different levels of care both for seniors and for younger people who were experiencing a variety of ailments. I also began to see the benefits of being involved with the community that exists in a long-term care home. In many cases clients actually improved when they moved out of their own homes and into a facility. They went in kicking and screaming, but three months later they were happy, relaxed, and had improved health. Their medication was now being monitored and they did not have to provide the day-to-day maintenance living alone requires.

My father's father had Alzheimer's disease in the later years of his life. My mother and father felt that it was best to keep him in his own home with round-the-clock care. My grandfather had been an outgoing and likeable individual. He had been reeve of the town and president of Rotary. But life changed after he developed Alzheimer's. When he was left in his own home with two women who were often frustrated with him, his character became completely different. They fed him, cleaned the house, and tried to protect him from harming himself, but he was left craving stimulation and a connection to people other than his caregivers and a few family members. He needed a community. My mother sees now, after hearing my research and the stories that others have told me, that he would have been better in a long-term care home where he could have interacted with a variety of people each day and been involved in numerous programs.

On the other hand, my late uncle, who had been a well-known criminal lawyer and a Crown attorney, had Alzheimer's disease too. He lived in a nursing home and had a caregiver that the family hired to spend time with him and give him additional care. His wife remained living in the family home, and she had a caregiver with her. But they were fortunate that they could afford the additional help. Not everyone can.

In another situation, I had a client who lived with her husband until he passed away. At that time she insisted that her daughter resign from her job as a dental hygienist, move in with her, and become her full-time caregiver. The daughter's entire life now revolves around her mother's care. She never married and has no children, and her mother is the focus of her life. Although previously a happy person, she now suffers from depression and is on medication. She has also gained a lot of weight and has become a heavy smoker. There is a chance that the mother may outlive her daughter.

These situations made me ask the question, Are long-term care homes a better solution to some difficult problems? At the same time as I was working at St. Clair West Services for Seniors, there was a question that was very much on my mind. Why do some people age with a healthy attitude while others become depressed and despondent, even when they all have problems related to aging? This question has been the basis of my research for the last twenty years, and the answer to it was the foundation of my first book. As a baby boomer, I questioned how I could age with grace, dignity, and purpose, accepting the losses and changes that aging presents to everyone without becoming bitter.

I recall a situation where a woman was caring for her husband, who had Alzheimer's disease, yet she was calm and joyous. Why was she happy while others with far fewer problems were experiencing depression? This question ultimately led to years of research. I realized that for seniors who have an involved family and proper personal and medical care, remaining in their own home can be a good option, but for people who need more care and socialization long-term care may be a good answer.

While I was working at St. Clair West Services for Seniors, I presented papers at the Ontario Gerontology Association (OGA) and at the Fourth Global Conference of the International Federation on Aging. For the OGA, I talked about seven seniors who were aging with a healthy attitude despite life's difficulties, and for the Fourth Global Conference I photographed the seven seniors and took the photos to the conference. The people attending the session were intrigued by the presentation and loved the photos. Having been a tapestry weaver for twenty-five years, turning to the camera was a logical progression. This is where my love of photography and my love of working with seniors became united.

With the initial seven photographs, I had an exhibit at the Koffler Logia Gallery. Next, I had an exhibit at the Holy Blossom Temple in the Cecil and Harry Pearl Gallery, and the legendary Oscar Peterson came out with his wife, Kelly. Oscar gave a talk on "Creativity and Aging." Then there was a showing at the Rotunda in the Toronto City Hall.

For my first book, I tried to find someone who was living in a long-term care home and was very satisfied with his or her life there. I did not have to search very hard. One day, when I was outside tending to my beautiful perennial garden, a woman passed by and we started to chat. She told me about her mother-in-law, Ann Seaton, who was happily living at the Apotex Centre Jewish Home for the Aged at the Baycrest.

As I was beginning to interview Ann for my first book, she said, "I'm still excited with living! Each day is a gift to treasure and use. I have a great desire to live, not just to exist. I'm not ready to let go yet. I'm curious about what will happen next — to my family, to me, and to the world. These are some of the best years of my life — I am having a wonderful time. Without responsibilities from managing a house I am free to explore life."[1] Ann went to the symphony, ballet, lectures, etc., with the help of Wheel Trans. She was confined to a motorized scooter, as she suffered from congenital dislocation of both hips and had had a stroke, but this did not slow her down.

Something Ann said to me made so much sense. She said that when she was young she had many friends, and when she grew older, married, and had children they lost touch due to their many responsibilities. Now, at the end of her life, she has met several people in the nursing home whom she knew when she was young. She laughed and said, "At the end of our lives, we are together again."

After three exhibits and my book *Treasured Legacies: Older and Still Great*, I approached Gilbert Heffern. Because of Ann's powerful thoughts and words I wanted to find out more about the positive side of life in a long-term care facility.

I found that people living in nursing homes were forgotten and had become invisible to society. Anything is

sexier than aging in a nursing home, yet the reality is that with the support the home provides, many residents continue to pursue personal interests, activities, and relationships that give meaning and quality to their lives. (One woman I interviewed said her health improved when she moved to a long-term care home with her husband, as she now has the care she requires right at hand and has exercise equipment right on their floor in the home — she described it as having a second chance at life.)

With the support and backing of Gilbert Heffern and the Ontario Long Term Care Association, I began to travel around the province and find people who were living in nursing homes and were finding joy, purpose, and meaning in their lives. Hopefully this book will bring presence and dignity to people who are in long-term health facilities.

Below I have listed some of the thoughts that were shared with me in my journey regarding nursing homes. The voices of the residents themselves stand in stark contrast to the first comment below, which reflects the general sterotypical view that one often hears in passing:

- "Shoot me in the head, kill me, but don't put me in a nursing home." (This was said to me by a colleague of my husband's, who is also a lawyer.)
- "I felt so guilty that my children were worried about me much of the time, and they felt guilty suggesting that I may be better living in a long-term care facility — now that I am here I see that it was the right decision. I no longer feel that I am draining my children of their energy that they need for their own children and their work, and

1. Irene Borins Ash, *Treasured Legacies: Older & Still Great* (Toronto: Second Story Press, 2003), 56.

they no longer feel guilty by suggesting that a home may be a positive option."

- "As a teenager I began to paint, but difficult times in history, marriage, responsibilities got in the way. Now at eighty-six years of age and with 10 percent vision in one eye I finally have the time to create the paintings that I had only imagined in my head. I will leave these paintings to my family as a legacy. I try to make each painting better than the last one. It is a challenge and worth waking up each day for. I am still alive!"

- "I needed more care than my aging wife could provide. My care was compromising her health. Now I receive the care I require by living in a long-term care home, and she lives in our family home. Her health has improved and she visits every day, often with some of our children and grandchildren."

- "Sylvia and I have always loved each other. Now she has Alzheimer's disease, and we waited until we could go into a long-term care home together. We've been married for sixty-three years, and I wouldn't leave Sylvia for anything. Now I realize we should have done this ten years ago. Why did we wait so long? We have meals, activities, outings. This is like a hotel. It is like being on a cruise."

- "I was afraid to go into a long-term care home because of the awful negative reputation that they have. Now that I am here I see I was wrong. It was the image I was afraid of, not the reality. Before going in I believed that it would be like living a life in a prison or monastery."

- "My wife died a few months ago. If we had not moved to a long-term care home I would have been afraid to face her impending death while we were living in our own home. Now I am trying to get used to living without her. I am finding that with support from the family and from the staff I am gradually getting over the loss and starting to live again."

- "I do not want to be a burden to our children — they have their own responsibilities and their own lives to live. By moving to a long-term care home our children's minds are more at peace, as they were always worried about us. Now they know we are being cared for. And they visit us and take us out to their home for dinner every week. We go on outings together. We talk on the phone daily. Life is better like this for everyone involved."

- "Death can be frightening, but being in a long-term care home makes this issue less overwhelming as there is staff to talk to, and sometimes other residents. My family hired a Personal Support Worker to be with me a few hours each day. She has become a friend. She listens to me. I am not as afraid as I used to be when the end comes."

- "People who were never married or who were married but never had children have fewer supports, and a long-term care home offers medical care, activities, and a chance to socialize. The home has become my community. I like it here. But it took time. I was unsure at the beginning, but it is fine now."

- "Religion has helped me deal with the changes and the losses in life. There are clergy at the home I live in and services that I attend. This helps me cope and brings me inner peace in my later years."

- "I never thought I'd learn to use a computer. But while living in a long-term care home I am sending emails to my children, grandchildren, and friends. I'm so proud."

- "I find that the exercise equipment, activities, outings, movies, and holiday celebrations are very enjoyable. I just turned 104, and with the help of a special staff member I started a writing career at 98. I won a prize for a poem that I wrote."

- "I used to volunteer when I was younger. A schoolteacher asked if some of the seniors at our long-term care home would come out and teach the schoolchildren to read. I am involved in this program that runs every week. I have actually made a friend of a young girl. I am another grandfather to her — and a special friend."

- "I am sixty-two and have had cerebral palsy since birth. By living in a supportive environment and with the help of Wheel Trans I am able to go out into the community alone. I go to movies, stores, and visit friends and family. With support, I am able to live a life like other people. I am independent, and I feel proud of my accomplishments."

Part I

PROFILES OF RESIDENTS IN LONG-TERM CARE

Profile 1

~

NIKOLA VASIC

Nikola Vasic painting in his room at Leisureworld Caregiving Centre, O'Connor Court, Toronto.

Nikola Vasic

Lieutenant in the Yugoslavian army, interior designer, artist, husband, father, and grandfather.

Born: Bagrden, Yugoslavia, 1920
Home: Leisureworld Caregiving Centre, O'Connor Court, Toronto

IT ALL BEGINS AT HOME

"I believe that making the world a better place begins at home. All of humanity must learn proper values and teach these values to our children. I value decent work, making an honest living, accumulating knowledge, and using this knowledge wisely. Every human being wants to strive to be better. I have a firm belief in God that has helped me through the difficult times."

I believe it is important to:

- "Believe in God"
- "Exercise and use one's creativity"
- "Remain connected to family"
- "Maintain a strong foundation of values"
- "Retain a healthy sense of optimism"
- "Have the freedom to pursue one's passions while living in a safe and supportive environment"

November 2006

History: Lieutenant in the Yugoslavian army, interior designer, artist, husband, father, grandfather

Born: Bagrden, Yugoslavia, 1920

Currently resident at: Leisureworld Caregiving Centre — O'Connor Court, Toronto

Keys to enjoying his later years: belief in God; exercising; creativity; connection to family; a foundation of values; a healthy sense of optimism

Why in a long-term care home: Need for assistance due to various infirmities; the freedom to pursue his passion

≈

Nikola grew up in Yugoslavia at a very difficult and uncertain time. When he was old enough, he joined the navy and became a lieutenant. During the Second World War, from 1941 to 1945, he was in a German prison camp. When the war ended, Nikola decided not to return to Yugoslavia as the communists were in power. Feeling it was time to start a new life, Nikola went to Belgium, where he found work as a coal miner and met his wife, Natalie. Together they had two daughters, Aleksandra and Lana.

In 1951, Nikola and his family left Europe and moved to Toronto, Canada. The only job he could find in his new country was washing floors. In his spare time, he began to study so that he could create a better life for himself and his family.

Nikola says his life has been a creative journey: he started to paint in high school, and ever since he has spent much of his free time reading to expand his artistic knowledge.

In Toronto, Nikola's natural talent for design emerged, and in time he became an interior designer, starting his own company, Impeccable Decorating Company, with a staff of twelve. He was finally able to earn a good living for his family while also pursuing his passion for creativity.

Before moving to Leisureworld Caregiving Centre — O'Connor Court a few years ago, Nikola found very little time to paint. His goal was to resume painting, as he now had the time. His daughter Aleksandra supplies him with the acrylic paint, the canvases, and the paintbrushes. Nikola feels that his painting style has improved and he is becoming a better, more precise painter. Although he has no vision in one eye and only 10 percent in the other eye, he is still able to create very beautiful paintings. For Nikola, this time in his life is a new beginning — a time to do some of his most creative work.

Nikola feels at peace with his decision to move into a long-term care home because of his various medical conditions. When he was nineteen, he had an accident that damaged his ability to control his balance. Because of this worsening condition, he has been confined to a wheelchair for the past seven and a half years. As a diabetic, he has his illness monitored daily by the nursing staff in his residence. Because of these ailments, it would be difficult for his wife, Natalie, to assist him in a home setting. Still, he maintains his close family connections: he sees his wife, daughters, and the rest of the family on a regular basis. He especially enjoys the frequent occasions on which his daughters bring him to their homes.

Nikola is able to maintain his mobility and strength by exercising for an hour on his own every day and by going for physiotherapy several times a week in the residence.

A firm belief in God has helped him through the difficult times. He feels that the intricacy and the beauty of the universe instill within him an unshakeable faith that there is a God.

Nikola explained that what matters to him most now is his family and becoming a better painter. He regards himself as an optimist and continues to find joy in his life.

Profile 2

∽

RONALD PONSFORD

Ronald Ponsford doing woodwork in a special workshop area prepared for him at Wellesley Central Place, Toronto.

Ronald Ponsford

Sailor in British Merchant Navy, traveller, restaurateur, wood carver, husband, father, grandfather, and volunteer.

Born: Cardiff, U.K., 1934
Home: Wellesley Central Place, Toronto

LEARN FROM PAST MISTAKES

"We should forsake greed and its many manifestations such as violence and war. If I were younger and was drafted to go to war, I would be a conscientious objector. I find it sad that people have not learned from their past mistakes."

I believe it is important to:

- "Follow my passion for woodworking"
- "Learn new skills such as using the computer"
- "Maintain family ties"
- "Make the most of every situation"
- "Obtain assistance when needed to support aging"

January 2007

History: Sailor in British Merchant Navy, traveller, restaurateur, woodcarver, husband, father, grandfather, volunteer

Born: Cardiff, South Wales, 1934

Currently resident at: Wellesley Central Place, Toronto, Ontario

Keys to enjoying his later years: Following his passion for woodworking; learning new skills such as using the computer; keeping family ties; making the most of every situation

Why in a long-term care home: affordability; proximity to previous residence; need for assistance as a result of various infirmities; freedom to pursue his passions; support and routines to reduce his fear of aging and of death

⌁

Ronald was raised primarily by his grandmother, as his mother was busy working to help support the family. He finished public school at the age of fourteen, and he joined the British Merchant Navy at seventeen. During his service, he travelled to many places, including France, Spain, Cuba, Newfoundland, and all across the United States.

While Ronald was in Boston he left the navy and went to Ellis Island, off New York City, where he remained in a holding centre for two months. He was sent back to Wales and enlisted in the British Army for two years. At the end of the enlistment, deciding it was time to settle down, he married his childhood sweetheart, Patricia. They had two children: a son, Raymond, and a daughter, Eileen.

Ronald always aspired to be a cabinetmaker but needed to take whatever work he could find, namely factory and foundry work.

Patricia and Ronald opened a restaurant in Cardiff and operated it for sixteen years, working long, hard hours. When they were ready to leave Wales, Patricia's sister — who was living in Scarborough — sponsored the family, enabling them to come to Canada. While spending time in Newfoundland, Ronald had decided that Canada would be a good place to live.

Ronald and Patricia found work in Hamilton as the superintendents of a three-hundred-unit apartment building. Their efforts paid off, as they were able to purchase their own home. After selling their house, they moved to Toronto to be closer to their daughter.

As Patricia grew older, she faced several health challenges, including a hip replacement and two back surgeries. In addition, both Patricia and Ronald became insulin-dependent diabetics.

While the couple lived in their home, nurses came three times a week to help Patricia. However, it was becoming increasingly difficult for them to remain living on their own. Ronald had to maintain the house, shop, and help Patricia with her medication, as well as administer his own. They moved to Wellesley Central Place, as it was affordable and close to where they had lived, offering them a familiar neighbourhood.

Ronald said he found meaning in his life while living in a long-term care home by helping to care for his wife until she passed away. Prior to her death they lived in separate rooms within the same home, as their needs were different. Immediately after Patricia's death he began to work on the grieving process.

Ronald is finally taking the time to work with wood, finding great pleasure in carving beautiful birds. He has rediscovered and expressed his artistic side in his senior years. Ronald likens the long-term care home to a hotel, saying that it provides the best situation for his current needs. Knowing that he is well cared for alleviates his family's constant concern for his safety and well-being.

Ronald remarks that aging can be frightening and being in a long-term care home helps to allay some of this fear. He still looks forward to each day for the opportunity to see his children and grandchildren. He is also grateful to breathe the fresh air every day. Although not spiritual or religious, he prevails because of his love for his wife, children, and grandchildren. He is happy to continuing woodcarving, learning the computer, and pursuing various types of study.

He believes that we can make the world a better place. We should forsake greed and its many manifestations. For example, he did not support the war in Iraq and finds American policy historically greedy, as exemplified by the United States importing coal from Wales at a cheap price in order to keep their own coal.

Profile 3

NORVAL E. TOOKE

Norval E. Tooke in his room using his computer and watching his big-screen TV at Kensington Health Centre, Toronto.

Norval E. Tooke

Insurance company manager and traveller.

Born: Toronto, Ontario, Canada, 1925
Home: Kensington Health Centre, Toronto

AVOCATIONS AS LABOURS OF LOVE

"I believe everyone should carry a sincere avocation with them throughout their adult life: something they truly enjoy doing or performing, but which does not necessarily lead to monetary gain. I am thinking of things such as playing piano, bird watching, being an opera buff, or restoring antique cars. The selection palette is broad and varied. However, any such choice should not be dabbled in, but should be wallowed in as a labour of love. If one makes the appropriate choice, the joie de vivre unconsciously gained is a lifeline that will enable them to better cope with the hard knocks that life in their future certainly will offer them."

I believe it is important to:

- "Use the extra time available to organize life"
- "Seek to understand oneself and others better"
- "Accept one's current limitations"
- "Indulge in one's interests, such as arts and culture"
- "Take the opportunities to interact and socialize with other residents and staff"

November 2006

History: Insurance company manager, traveller

Born: Toronto, Ontario, 1925

Currently resident at: Kensington Health Centre, Toronto, Ontario

Keys to enjoying his later years: Using the extra time available to organize his life; understanding himself and others better; accepting his current limitations; indulging his interest in arts and culture

Why in a long-term care home: Having the needed support to deal with the physical infirmities that developed after his stroke; socializing with other residents and staff

---

Norval's Swedish mother, Anna Johnson, was born in 1887. She left her birth country in 1903, arriving in the United States through Ellis Island. Anna became a travelling companion to a wealthy older woman, with whom she travelled extensively and elegantly. Anna was exposed to art and culture and developed a passion for travel — pleasures that Norval was drawn to as he grew older.

Anna moved to Toronto in 1917, where she met her husband, Ray, upon his return from the First World War in 1919. They had two children, but their first child, Norval's sister, died suddenly and unexpectedly at the age of two, just prior to his birth. As a result of this terrible loss, his parents were overprotective of him as a child, keeping him from interacting with other children. He grew up in a world of adult relatives with their Victorian and Edwardian behavioural rules. This upbringing eventually led him to become independent, but also made him the introverted loner he now feels he is.

Once in high school, Norval began working part-time after school and on weekends clerking in a local grocery store. He kept this job for seven years, well into his university career. His summer months were spent on a family dairy farm doing various chores: his favourite task was rounding up the cattle at milking time with a trained cattle dog called Riley, who knew more about the proper technique that Norval did. Obviously, Norval and Riley became pals.

Norval's stint at the University of Toronto was important, as the knowledge he gained there remained with him throughout his life and shaped his insights, as well as his fondness for the arts and sciences. He believes that his education opened his mind to readily accepting broader concepts and ideas.

While still in high school, the money from his part-time job enabled him to explore New York City and the New England area. Later, when fully employed, he spent his holidays in various parts of Europe sightseeing, seeking out flea markets, bistros, and pubs, and viewing the occasional concert or opera at performing arts centres.

Norval never married, and at times he felt isolated. He craved activity and interaction with others. Throughout his life, whether in Toronto or while travelling, Norval would find a bistro or pub that he enjoyed and would return to it again and again. While there, he would do crossword puzzles and read the paper. Over time he would be treated as a regular, and people started to talk with him on a deeper level. Norval would drink beer or scotch throughout the day, but he never had a problem with alcohol. The pub was his outlet for socializing.

Working for one company (Crown Life Insurance) for his entire career would make Norval somewhat of a rarity in today's world. Nonetheless, his long tenure there had its rewards. At one point he was sent to London, England, to manage an administrative office in the company's British operation. He remained in England for seven years. When computer usage was in its infancy, he was involved in data processing, eventually becoming a manager of the corporation's data processing division in Canada.

In 1985, Norval was diagnosed with Type 2 diabetes and became insulin dependent. His immediate symptoms were double vision and feeling physically ill. His vision was so badly affected that for a time he was diagnosed as being legally blind. Norval received hospital counselling in living with and controlling the disease and was advised to lose weight and to strictly adhere to a prescribed diet. He faithfully followed this advice, and after requiring insulin for two years, he gradually decreased his need for it, after which he went into remission. He remains insulin-free to this day.

When asked why he finally moved to a long-term care home, Norval replied, "Prior to March 17, 2004, I lived in my own home, looked after myself, used public transportation, and depended on no one else. Then the stroke! Almost a year later, when it became time to leave the rehabilitation facility and move on, the choice had to be a long-term care home because I could not walk or transfer myself from one place to another [i.e., from chair to bed, etc.]. In other words, I could not go home, and Kensington was the best solution."

When Norval first realized he needed to move into a long-term care home, he pictured it as an institution, much like prison or a monastery with his room as a cell. Gradually, he has found meaning and interest in his life in the home. Having a computer in his room and a large-screen television helps keep his mind active. He also reads several newspapers daily, does crossword puzzles, and plays computer card games. Various friends visit him on a regular basis.

When asked about the positive aspects of aging, Norval said that as he is approaching the end of his life his goal is to organize himself well enough to be able to cope with the tribulations and clutter arising from day-to-day living. The downside is dealing with the physical problems he faces with aging. His philosophy is to learn to accept what lies ahead. Problems are a challenge that one should try to solve. As he has grown older, he has a greater understanding of the problems he has faced throughout his life and the problems others have experienced. He questions more at this time in his life than when he was younger.

Reflecting back on his journey, Norval says that he regrets not pursuing his love of both music and education.

"By the age of twelve or thirteen, with one foot testing adulthood, most people have an idea of what they would like to do as far as career is concerned. If they choose a profession and steer their studies in that direction, the further they progress, the more firmly they cement that choice. Ergo, their future life is set," he said. "If, on the other hand, they don't pre-select their future high school and university subjects, they find themselves on the job market as fodder for any hiring company and end up performing random functions as decided by the company. I believe everyone should carry a sincere avocation with them throughout their adult life. In my case, I would choose the piano and work to develop my playing ability as close to a concert level as possible. Then I could rely on a Chopin waltz or etude or even a Joplin rag to express joy, or a piano rendition of a Wagner opus to express my other feelings."

Profile 4

ELEANOR G. MUNRO

Personal support worker Beth Rodrigo (left) polishes Eleanor Munro's nails
in her room at Kensington Health Centre, Toronto.

Eleanor G. Munro

University of Toronto graduate with a B.A., office worker, sales person, volunteer, avid reader, bridge player, mother, and grandmother.

Born: Star City, Saskatchewan, Canada, 1921
Home: Kensington Health Centre, Toronto

LIFELONG GIFTS FROM OTHERS

"I acknowledge the influence of my parents and husband, as well as my many close friends, in developing my positive outlook on life I have always been concerned about others and especially those less fortunate than I have been throughout my life. My advice to people younger than myself: Try to take care of other people and do not be too wrapped up with yourself."

I believe it is important to:

- "Maintain a positive attitude to life"
- "Be concerned about others"
- "Be open to receiving family support"
- "Believe in God"
- "Always stay involved and socialize with others"

January 2007

History: University of Toronto graduate with a B.A., office worker, salesperson, volunteer, avid reader, bridge player, mother, grandmother

Born: Star City, Saskatchewan, 1921

Currently resident at: Kensington Health Centre, Toronto, Ontario

Keys to enjoying her later years: Support from her family and friends; attending church services; helping others (especially those less fortunate than herself); maintaining a positive outlook on life; being grateful for what life has offered

Why in a long-term care home: Support required due to her arthritis; routine and schedule of services provided; having a private room

Eleanor spent the first two years of her life in Star City, Saskatchewan, and then the family lived in Swift Current, where they stayed until they moved to Toronto when Eleanor was seventeen. She attended high school in Toronto and then studied at the University of Toronto. She married her husband, Bain, in 1944, and they had four children in six years.

After studying law, Eleanor's husband went into private practice in Cayuga and then Hagersville, a town close to Hamilton, Ontario. Eleanor was kept very busy raising four young children.

As the children became more independent, Eleanor began volunteer work and also became involved in sales and office work.

Bain was the director of a Legal Aid office until he died at age seventy-five. Eleanor lived on her own following Bain's death until she developed arthritis. Up until this time, she had been able to live on her own safely, but as she became more arthritic she required more care, which was too expensive and unavailable in her small town.

Eleanor is enjoying her life at Kensington Health Centre: she feels fortunate to be living there and to have her own private room. When asked about whether she finds life in a long-term care home fulfilling, she remarks that so much depends on one's attitude — and her outlook assures her a peaceful, calm life in her later years. She has always been grateful for what life has offered her. She also attends church services weekly in the facility.

Eleanor feels that she is receiving valuable support and opportunities to socialize with other residents — not as easily attainable if she were living in her own home. She likes the routine and the schedule that life in a long-term care home provides. For instance, she attends a daily exercise program at the residence, and also receives physiotherapy three times a week (an extra service enabled by her family). Eleanor also benefits from — and became friends with — Elizabeth Rodrigo, who helps her wash and style her hair and gives her manicures amongst other duties as a Personal Support Worker.

Eleanor is in constant touch with her family. Her three children who live in the Toronto area (Ross, Ken, and Mary) are in regular contact with her, in person or by phone; Mary tries to visit her daily. Her daughter Catharine, who lives in Western Canada, maintains frequent contact by phone.

Elizabeth Rodrigo

Nurse, PSW, personal caregiver to Eleanor Munro and others, wife and mother.

Born: Manila, Philippines, 1959

LESSONS IN COMPASSION AND WISDOM

"Working with seniors has taught me compassion, wisdom and how to care for people until the last moments of their life. I promised my residents I would be there with them until the end — which I was for each of them — as we had developed a very close relationship of trust and friendship. I often have music on so that the environment is calm and peaceful."

I believe it is important to:

- "Maintain a positive attitude to life"
- "Learn compassion and wisdom and caring for others"
- "Develop close relationships of trust and friendship with those I care for"

February 2007

History: Nurse, Personal Support Worker, personal caregiver to Eleanor Munro and others, wife, mother

Born: Manila, Philippines, 1959

＝

Elizabeth is one of four children. She had two sisters and one brother.

She studied nursing in the Philippines for four years and then moved to Saudi Arabia to practise nursing from 1987 to 1995. She became a nurse specializing in obstetrics and gynecology and did some midwifery work. She also married there.

Beth and Allan, her husband, moved to Canada in 1995. Beth went back to school, attending the Para-Med Academy to become a Personal Support Worker. She had a daughter, Areej, while living in Toronto. Beth was able to have her young daughter with her while she was caring for an elderly woman, Teresa Edwards, from 1995 until she passed away in 2000.

Next she worked at Chester Village as a private caregiver from 1998 to 2002. At the present time she helps three or four residents at Kensington Health Centre as a private caregiver, providing care for people who are bedridden. She feeds them, assists with bathing, does their hair and fingernails, and gives them whatever extra help they require.

When someone has Alzheimer's disease she uses touch and her voice so that they are aware of her presence. Often when she is off duty the family will come and spend time with their parent. People can die with dignity rather then dying alone.

Beth finds this work very rewarding as she took care of people as a young girl and somehow she always knew that caring for elderly people would be her calling. She would by far prefer to be a Personal Support Worker than a nurse as she has rewarding one on one time with the clients. She wants to become attached to the clients. She and Eleanor have become close friends.

Beth found that she became depressed a while ago after three patients that she was caring for died all in a short span. She received support from her parents, husband, and Eleanor to help her through this difficult time. Her depression did not affect her clients.

She had a bad impression of long-term care homes at the beginning, but now she sees that they are the best solution for both the patients and the family.

Profile 5

〰

IRENE GREENBLOOM

Irene Greenbloom in her room, surrounded by the paintings she creates in the art studio at Baycrest in Toronto.
Many residents at Baycrest work in the large studio, which is located on the ground floor.

Irene Greenbloom

Artist, Holocaust survivor, mother, grandmother, mother-in-law.

Born: Lodz, Poland, 1914
Home: Baycrest Centre for Geriatric Care, Toronto

EVERYONE IS CREATED EQUAL

"My mother taught me that it is more important to be a good person than to be religious or observant. My husband and I taught our children to believe that everyone is created equal. I feel that it is important to help all people, regardless of their background, and that anti-Semitism and racism in general are at the root of the problems in the world today."

I believe it is important to:

- "Keep up with the events of the world"
- "Enjoy support from family and friends"
- "Continue to learn"
- "Observe the joy my painting brings to others"

January 2007

History: Artist, Holocaust survivor, mother, grand-mother, mother-in-law

Born: Lodz, Poland, 1914

Currently resident at: Baycrest Centre for Geriatric Care, Toronto, Ontario

Keys to enjoying her later years: Keeping up with the events of the world; having support from her family and friends; continuing to learn; painting and observing the joy it brings to others

Why in a long-term care home: Physical and emotional support from the staff; the comfort of feeling safe

~~~

Irene Greenbloom (née Weinberger) was born in Lodz, Poland, in 1914. Because of the war, her parents moved with Irene and her brother, Mike, to Russia in 1917, where the siblings spent their childhood in Dnepropetrovsk. Some time after the revolution in Russia, the family returned to Poland. Irene explains that the situation in Poland was terrible, due to increasing anti-Semitism. Two of her uncles and her grandfather were killed when the family journeyed from Russia to Poland. Once they arrived there, her parents had to start life over again.

Irene enjoyed high school, where she had many friends and took private art classes. After graduating from high school, she went to France, studying bacteriology and art at the Beaux Art School.

Irene met her husband, Zigmund Felzen (also Polish), in France. After he studied medicine, they returned to Poland. They were married there, and soon after Irene became pregnant. Her husband fled to Russia with her brother due to the rise of Nazism, but Irene stayed with her parents in Poland because of her pregnancy. Tragically, her husband was killed in the hospital where he was working in Russia when the Germans took control. He never saw their son, George, who was born in the Lodz ghetto that Germans established after they overran the city.

When George was young, Irene would paint dogs and birds to show him, as there were no dogs and very little beauty in the ghetto. Life was hard, with all the occupants filled with fear for their very existence. When the ghetto was liquidated, Irene was sent to Auschwitz with George. After the Nazis took her away to work as a greeting card artist, her parents and son disappeared. She never saw them again, as they were sent to the furnaces.

Irene worked in a linen factory until the end of the war and did drawings for the Germans. She was able to survive because she was useful to the Germans with her artistic skills and her ability to speak several languages. She saved the lives of two other women as she said she needed help to produce the greeting cards. Yet she still suffered, as she was cold and hungry most of the time. The key lesson she learned during the war was to learn whatever you can as everything will be useful over the course of your lifetime.

Following the war, in 1947, Irene went back to Lodz to search for any living family members or others she knew. She was unable to find anyone. When she returned to her home, someone else was living there, and she was forced to leave everything behind.

Irene met her second husband, Jacob, when they were both searching for any lost family members. Jacob had lost his wife, two children, and five siblings but had been saved by the actions of Oskar Schindler. To this day, Irene still remembers how her husband was saved by a German.

Jacob and Irene were married in Poland, and their daughter, Mary, was born there. Following the war, Jacob kept looking for any family members who might have survived the war. He had some second cousins who lived in Toronto and New York. Their family purchased tickets for them to leave Europe and come to the United States in search of a better life; they entered through Ellis Island.

After leaving New York and moving to Toronto, Jacob worked in a fur factory until he started his own business. He owned and operated a factory where fireproof doors were made for buildings. They had another child, David.

When Jacob began to work in Canada he never forgot what Oskar Schindler had done for so many people, and he and a few friends sent money to Schindler, who had depleted his money while trying to save the Jews.

The family worked very hard to assimilate into their new country, but remnants of their horrific Holocaust experiences continued to haunt them.

At the age of sixty-two, Jacob died of a heart attack. He had been a smoker. Irene sold the house and purchased a condominium where she lived with her son, David. During this time Irene began to attend a day program at Baycrest where she painted and became involved with other activities. She said that she had a very positive experience in the day program. When it was no longer safe to live in the condominium, she moved to Baycrest at the age of ninety-four as a full-time resident. Because of various infirmities, such as arthritis, she could no longer be on her own.

Despite the fact that Irene is blind in one eye, she paints every day, taking a break only on weekends. Her family, as well as a young friend, Lisa, and her dog, visit Irene regularly. When asked about the positive aspects of aging, Irene said that she is still very interested in the world around her and reads the newspaper daily. Every Friday she is taken by Wheel Trans to her daughter's home, where they celebrate the Sabbath, despite the fact that Irene lost her faith in God, as she could not understand a God that would let innocent people be killed in the camps. She is not kosher and does not go to synagogue.

Profile 6

MAE MERKLEY

Rosemary Merkley (left), "Care Bear" (centre), and Mae Merkley (right)
at Hillcrest Village Care Centre, Midland, Ontario.

Mae Merkley (née Contois)

Housewife, mother, grandmother, community and religious participant, storyteller, nanny, and worker at food plant.

Born: Lafontaine, Ontario, Canada, 1921
Home: Hillcrest Village Care Centre, Midland, Ontario

THE MOMENTS COUNT

"Mae's short term memory is almost non-existent so that you may visit her for two hours, and ten minutes after you have left she doesn't remember that you were there. It is most important to remember that the moments that you are there are comforting for her. She enjoys the time together. We need to remember that if she doesn't know one of us that WE KNOW HER and that is important for us. Just as you would visit a small child in a hospital who doesn't remember that you were there and wants you with them so that she can feel safe, it is the same for Mae now. This is very hard for us to see Mom like this and it is equally difficult for Mom to be in this state."

Rosemary Merkley R.N., daughter

Mom believed it is important to:

- "Have a strong belief in God"
- "Remain connected to family"
- "Know that she is not a burden to her family"

March 2007

History: Public school graduate, food plant worker, political volunteer, active church volunteer, skier and camper, storyteller, wife, mother, grandmother, great-grandmother

Born: Lafontaine, Ontario, 1921 (Mae Merkley passed away in 2008, during the editing of this book)

Resident at: Hillcrest Village Care Centre, Midland, Ontario

Keys to enjoying her later years: Support from her family, friends, and caregivers; listening to music; religion; treats; Jimmy (a white Care Bear)

Why in a long-term care home: Going to events in the home; having a safe and secure environment for her Alzheimer's disease; the relief of pain through a pain management schedule

As Mae had Alzheimer's, the text below was written by her daughter and constant caregiver, Rosemary Merkley, R.N.

~

Ella Mae Merkley (née Contois) was born in the family home in the small French village of Lafontaine, Ontario, on November 25, 1921. At the age of three she moved to Midland. She was a frail child, always smaller than her sister Rose, who was younger by twenty-one months. Mae had a special bond with her oldest sister. One of her siblings died at birth, and the others are as follows in order of age: Alma, Xavier, Alida, Herbie, Edna, Henry, Mae, Rose, Lavigna, Leona, Lionel, Marie, and Nelson.

Mae passed her Grade 8 exams; however, she wasn't allowed to go to high school as her mother needed her at home to help out. Months after graduating, she started working as a housekeeper and nanny. Even though Mae was separated from her family she gave them $8.00 out of the $10.00 she made each month. She had one day a week off and was not allowed to have anyone (family or friends) over to the houses she worked at. During these two jobs she learned how to keep an immaculately clean house and how to cook. Her husband and children certainly benefited in later years from these experiences.

Mae's first marriage was to Lawrence Legault. Lawrence and Mae had one daughter, Theresa. Lawrence was killed in the Second World War at the age of twenty-two, after which Mae and Theresa lived for a time with Lawrence's parents in Penetanguishene. They treated them very well. Mae then lived on her own in Midland with Theresa until Theresa was five years old.

In 1948 Mae met Cecil Merkley, a widower with a nine-year-old daughter, Ann. Cecil and Mae were married on December 28, 1948, at St. Margaret's Parish in Midland. Mae and Cecil had five daughters together between 1949 and 1963.

In 1954 the Midland Ship Yard closed. It was a large employer for Midland. Cecil, now out of work, went on his first Canadian Steamship Line (CSL) ship. He worked on the CSL ships until the late 1960s as a marine engineer. Cecil took courses to advance his education, and Mae would help him prepare for exams in the winter months by asking him sample questions until late in the night. Cecil then worked on the CPR passenger ships, the *Anninaboia* and the *Keewatin*, which came into Port McNicoll, a few miles from Midland. This was a time for a more natural family life together. After Cecil completed his 2nd Class Stationary Engineer papers, he got a job at the RCA plant in Midland.

These three jobs were life-changing experiences for the whole family. During the years that Cecil worked on the CSL ships it meant that he and Mae were apart for months at a time with only one- to three-day visits until the ship was laid up for two and a half months over the winter, during which Cecil would be home. This meant that Mae was on her own with the children, managing all of the household, child care, and financial matters in Cecil's absence. (She learned to drive a standard driven car in 1954, when Cecil began his work with the CSL and realized that he would not be home most of the time.) When Mae was sick at home or in hospital, Cecil would have to take over the household.

Mae was a very independent woman. She became a jack of all trades. She would wash and change storm windows and do all of the spring and fall cleaning, which consisted of washing all the walls and ceilings, painting, and making repairs as necessary. She could fix small appliances, hang a clothesline, cut the grass for a very large yard, do a little plumbing — basically, she wasn't held back from doing whatever was necessary around the home. She was doctor, nurse, teacher, counsellor, and friend. Learning how to sew was also an important asset.

Mae stayed at home full-time until their youngest child went to school. She started out working in a general store, sometimes bringing work home. After Cecil died in 1976, Mae worked full-time at the Pillsbury Plant in Midland while raising the last three teenage girls on her own … again.

Mae was very active in St. Margaret's Parish church and school activities, including the Catholic Women's League and the Church Extension Society, which knit hats, sweaters, and mittens for the poor. As the years went on this group of women started a card group that would last fifty years. Mae was a great pastry cook. Her butter tarts were so famous in Midland that when there was a church bake sale the women would watch out for Mae and often buy her tarts before they hit the table.

Mae enjoyed learning to cross-country ski in her sixties. She also enjoyed camping on Beausoleil Island for years with her children, and with Cecil once he had a stationary engineer position at RCA. Mae has been a mother and grandmother. She has eleven grandchildren and eight great-grandchildren. Mae's vocation in life has been to look after her family. It is a good thing that Mae was such a people person as she included all the families involved with her children from all three marriages (hers and Cecil's). As children we knew eight grandparents plus aunts, uncles, and cousins.

Mae's daughter Theresa lived with her for two years in an effort to keep her in her own home and as independent as possible. As Mae's care needs changed her daughter Rosemary moved in with her for another two and a half years. During these four and a half years her other children would help out as much as their health and family commitments allowed. Mae always said that she would not move in with family as she had seen how that arrangement had affected other family and friends. As time went on Mae's world became smaller and smaller. She went from being a social butterfly who needed an answering machine so her family could get in touch with her to spending her time in her own home.

She found it increasingly difficult to leave home because of physical limitations and mental changes. She felt safe in her own home, but as years went on Mae would have times when she wanted to go back to her childhood family home. She went through a period where her verbal skills were changing. She had several mini-strokes. She became frustrated until Jimmy came into her life at Christmas 2004.

Jimmy is a white Care Bear. He moves his arms and makes sounds like a young baby would, cooing and laughing. Mae always loved babies. Jimmy is sound-activated once you get him started by pressing on his foot. Jimmy has turned out to be a godsend as he keeps her company.

As Mae's cognitive impairment grew worse she moved to Hillcrest Village in April 2005.

Mae's faith has been a source of comfort and strength to her. She used to watch *Daily Mass* on TV and say the prayers she learned as a child, if she had someone to pray with her. She could not have survived her life without her relationship with God. Right now she walks well. In the long-term care home Mae sits with other residents. She takes part in some of the activities if she is brought to them. She prefers to be with one to two people at a time and needs encouragement as well as help to participate in conversations.

She comes out with the funniest things and can at times say what is in her heart, for example "I am looking forward to you coming to visit. It is lonely sometimes."

Mae is a survivor. She has survived a knee replacement and hip fracture. Mae has severe pain due to osteoporosis and fractured vertebrae and arthritis. One of our main concerns was that her pain be managed well. She is on a pain medicine schedule that provides excellent pain relief. This is especially important for someone who is confused at times or whose verbal skills are compromised due to strokes or any other medical condition.

There are several things that make Mae's life better despite having Alzheimer's disease. A big one is visits from her daughters, as well as from her sisters and brother. Her oldest friend, Jean, continues to visit Mae at the long-term care home, as do her other her friends. She also has Helen, a caregiver and friend, who comes three or four evenings a week from 7:00 p.m. to 9:00 p.m. Helen gets her ready for bed, walks with her, and brings her treats, for example fresh-picked fruit and baking.

She enjoys going to events in the long-term care home with family or with Helen, for example Legion singers and musicians, hymn sings, a Christmas party with the Brownies, and picnics. Mae enjoys simple movies, Gaiter Gospel Hour on Friday nights, saying the rosary with someone, taking meals with the family, talks with the staff (especially when they sit down with her), foot massages, weekly visit from hospice volunteer Pat (who does her nails, reads to her, and looks at old family photos), and getting her hair styled every week and permed every three months. Sometimes Mom and I dance together, sing, pray, talk, or just sit together. I help her to interact and notice her surroundings. With seven children there are seven different ways to interact with Mom and to bring enjoyment into her life for the moment.

Profile 7

∽

DAVID AND SYLVIA CHADWICK

David and Sylvia Chadwick, still in love. Photo taken in their room at Extendicare Bayview, Toronto.

David Chadwick

Entrepreneur, kibbitzer, volunteer, father and grandfather.

Born: Toronto, Ontario, Canada, 1919
Home: Extendicare Bayview, Toronto

Sylvia Chadwick (née Sone)

Office worker, customer service surveyor, volunteer, piano player, mother, and grandmother.

Born: Toronto, Ontario, Canada, 1920
Home: Extendicare Bayview, Toronto

ACTING ON BELIEFS

"We believe in being kind and thoughtful to all people. People are all the same. It does not matter what their religious or ethnic background is. When we were travelling in the United States and there were separate bathrooms for blacks and whites we would use the black bathroom just to spite them!"

We believe it is important to:

- "Maintain a positive attitude and live in the present"
- "Be concerned about others"
- "Receive support from family"
- "Be together and socialize with others"
- "Avoid concerns about being a burden to family"

January 2007

History: David: Entrepreneur, kibitzer, volunteer, father, grandfather; Sylvia: Volunteer, housewife, part-time worker, piano player, mother, grandmother

Born: David: Toronto, Canada, 1919; Sylvia: Toronto, Canada, 1920

Currently resident in: Extendicare Bayview Nursing Home, Toronto, Ontario

Keys to enjoying their later years: Positive attitude to life; living in the present; being concerned about others; having support from and connections with their family, socializing with other residents; programs and food at the home

Why in a long-term care home: Physical, medical, and emotional support from the staff; concern about being a burden to their family; being in the home together

David Chadwick grew up in Toronto and went to Park Public School and Jarvis Collegiate High School. He went to Northern Vocational Business School for one year and then began to work for his father in a recycling business, M. Chadwick and Sons.

Sylvia Sone also grew up in Toronto. She attended Duke of York Public School and went to Jarvis Collegiate and then Northern Collegiate for one year. Sylvia loved to play the piano, and she met David at a party where she was playing. They were married in 1941 while

David was in the army. He was stationed variously at Camp Borden, in Nova Scotia, in Labrador, and in Toronto between 1942 and 1947.

Sylvia did office work before she was married. When their three children, Arlene, Harold, and Stephen, were growing up she was at home and very involved in their lives. Once the children were older she did surveys in shopping malls. She continued to play the piano, a great passion for her. She also volunteered for the Canadian Cancer Society, the Adath Israel Synagogue, and B'nai Brith. B'nai Brith is a Jewish volunteer and advocacy organization that is involved with anti-racism activities and encourages communication between people of diverse ethnic and social backgrounds and of all ages.

Sylvia and David loved to dance, and on the weekends they would hire a babysitter and go dancing with their friends. They thoroughly enjoyed each other's company, and this special quality in their relationship has remained with them to this day.

As Sylvia and David grew older they required some assistance to be able to live on their own. David had to do the cooking, shopping, and some of the housework as Sylvia had problems with her legs and also began showing signs of early Alzheimer's disease. They had services from Circle of Care, a community-based agency that provides services for people who are elderly or have disabilities and wish to remain in their own home.

David was having his own health issues. The problems began with a cataract operation and a stroke. David could have remained living on his own safely, with supports, but he did not want to be separated from Sylvia. They waited until they could go into the long-term care home at the same time. Another concern of David and Sylvia's was not to be a burden on their children.

When asked about their decision to come to a long-term care home they responded, "We should have been here twenty years ago!" They moved into the Extendicare Bayview Nursing Home in 2005. They did not own their own home but rather rented an apartment. They are able to pay for the long-term care home with their pensions.

When asked what they like about the long-term care home they live in, they said they like the food and the varied daily activities, especially bingo. They have assistance with showering. Sylvia is assisted with toilet use, which is important since it has become too hard for David to assist her as he is vision-impaired.

David and Sylvia speak to their daughter, Arlene, every day, and she visits once or twice a week. Stephen phones several times a week and visits often. Arlene has three children, and Stephen has two. Unfortunately David and Sylvia's son Harold passed away eight years ago. They attended services at the synagogue where they have been members for fifty years on Friday evenings but now attend services at the long-term care home. This is very important to them.

In the long-term care home they have their two beds pushed together. David said it is like being on a cruise. "I wouldn't leave Sylvia for anything. We want to be together. I've got Sylvia and she's got me."

David states that he has no unfinished business. He wakes up in the morning and feels happy and content. He feels that it is important to live in the present and not to worry about yesterday.

David never knew many members of his father's family as most of them perished in the Holocaust. But rather than feeling bitter he turned their life experiences to wisdom. David said that people should try to be tolerant and congenial. He feels that religion is the basis for all of the problems in the world today.

If people were more like the Chadwicks, the world would be a better place to live in.

Profile 8

~

EVELYN ROSEMUND WILLIAMS

Evelyn Rosemund Williams still has the same smile as the image taken of her at age seventeen (below), which hangs in her room at the Rekai Centre, Toronto.

Evelyn Rosemund Williams

Grade 10 graduate, housekeeping staff, wife, and mother.

Born: Toronto, Ontario, Canada, 1915
Home: Rekai Centre, Toronto

WHILE LYING IN MY HOSPITAL BED

"I do not feel too good today
Many thoughts going through my head
And in the midst of this
I try to pray in my hospital bed.
The sun is trying to shine on me
As if to take away some of my dread
And let my worries somehow flee
While lying in my hospital bed.
Love and kindness
Comes to mind
When I remember what the good book said
How strong faith brought sight to the blind
While lying in my hospital bed."

I believe it is important to:

- "Trust and believe in others"
- "Accept support from family, friends and staff"
- "Believe in God"
- "Learn new skills"

February 2007

History: Grade 10 graduate, wife, mother, housekeeping staff member

Born: Toronto, Ontario, 1915

Currently resident at: The Rekai Centre, Toronto

Keys to enjoying her later years: Support and visits from her family and friends; strong belief in God; learning new skills

Why in a long-term care home: Physical and emotional support from the staff; help in bathing; having a private room; the provision of care

~

Evelyn attended public school at Ryerson Public School. The family then moved to Etobicoke, and she finished Grade 10 at Long Branch High School. She had five siblings, Oliver, Bruce, Kenneth, Audrey, and Beaulah.

She left school after finishing Grade 10, as she had to help her parents. Her job was to clean private homes, spending most of the time on her hands and knees. In 1951, she got a job working at Lambert Lodge, a government-run long-term care home that today is called Christie Gardens.

Somewhere along the way, Evelyn decided that she had had enough of kneeling to clean floors, and one day she brought a mop to work. She told the management that she should not have to clean on her hands and knees. As a result of her persistence, the government regulations regarding housekeeping services at public-run facilities were changed, and all of the housekeeping staff members were afterwards allowed to use a mop to do their cleaning. Evelyn worked at Lambert Lodge for twenty-eight years.

Evelyn married Arthur Roy Williams in 1944. He had an automobile mechanic business, and Evelyn described him as being brilliant. Born in England to a white mother and a black father, he moved to Canada at the age of fifteen, leaving his family behind.

Evelyn and Arthur belonged to an organization called UNIA Hall, which other black people attended. They also belonged to an African Methodist Church. They loved gospel music and socializing with other church members.

After six years of marriage, Evelyn and Arthur divorced. Following the divorce, Evelyn lived alone with her young daughter, Armina. They lived in an apartment that was part of Metro Housing. When Armina moved out as an adult, Evelyn continued to live in the same apartment for many years.

Evelyn did not want to leave her apartment, but eventually she required more care. She has been living at the Rekai Centre for a year and a half in a private room, and she appreciates that she has help bathing. She finds the nurses who check on her well-being "tremendously nice and kind."

Evelyn sees her grandson and three great-grandchildren regularly, and is also visited by numerous family members and friends, including her brother, who takes her out every Saturday.

Recently Evelyn was hospitalized for high blood pressure. A firm believer in a loving God, she says that God keeps her going. She believes that God brought her out of her illness for a reason, which she feels may be to be a part of this project. Evelyn always wanted to record her life history, and she feels that fate brought us together so that her story would be told. Evelyn asked me what would happen if she passed away before the book was finished, and she was assured that no matter what she would be included in this project. Her story and her legacy need to be shared with others.

When asked how we can help make the world a better place she replied, "By trusting and believing in each other." She said that we should know that we do not stand alone because God is always there. When asked about what still matters to her she said that good friends matter. Some are gone now, but she always remembers them.

Evelyn is now learning to crochet from a volunteer visitor, brought in by her request. It is never too late to learn a new skill. She is making quilts out of the pieces that she crochets.

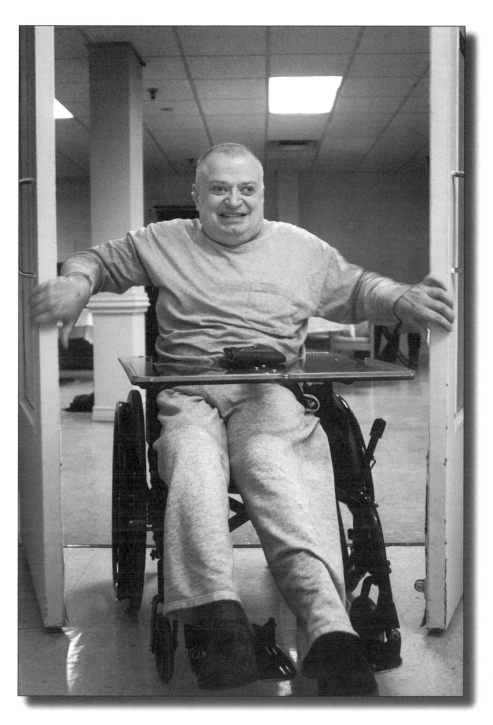

Profile 9

ZEV SELINGER

*Zev Selinger is seen going out the door at
Lincoln Place Nursing Home, Toronto.
Zev has an active life with family and friends
outside of Lincoln Place.*

Zev Selinger

Son, uncle, writer, and adventurer.

Born: Montreal, Quebec, Canada, 1944
Home: Lincoln Place Nursing Home, Toronto

THERE IS A COMMUNITY HERE

"Lincoln Place Nursing Home is located in the Forest Hill area of Toronto. I have been living here since October 2002. I enjoy life here very much. There is an Orthodox synagogue in the building where the full range of Jewish life takes place during the year. The food in the kitchen is Kosher and is very tasty. Activities such as bingo, Tai Chi, art therapy and special events such as Talent Shows [allow] the residents [to] express themselves artistically. I wish to mention my observation about the building itself. It is built in such a way that one cannot help but meet other people. This is really good because one does not feel lonely."

I believe it is important to:

- "Keep up with the events of the world"
- "Visit with family and friends"
- "Continue to learn"
- "Have feelings of connectedness, community and independence"

March 2007

History: son, uncle, writer, traveller

Born: Montreal, Quebec, 1944

Currently resident at: Lincoln Place Nursing Home, Toronto, Ontario

Keys to enjoying his later years: Keeping up with the events of the world; having support from and visiting with his family and friends; continuing to learn

Why in a long-term care home: Physical and emotional support from the staff; multiple programs; the feeling of connectivity, community, and independence

~

Zev was born the youngest son of Dr. Zelig Selinger. His brother, Yahudah, was born in 1942. Zev's father was a psychiatrist and a respected man in the community. Zev was born prematurely, and he had cerebral palsy. As he developed he found it very difficult to move his muscles. Up to the age of five he lived with his family. He left for the United States in 1950 and returned to Canada for good in 1954. Between 1950 and 1954 he went to two institutions for children with cerebral palsy, one in Jamestown, North Dakota, and one in Baltimore, Maryland.

In both facilities he was seen by specialists who helped him to develop his muscles. When he returned home in 1954 he was assessed for education, and at the age of ten was put into Grade 3. From grades 3 to 6 he went to regular school. Zev failed Grade 6. From grades 6 to 12 he attended a special needs school.

Zev wore leg braces from age five to age nineteen. In the house where his family lived he was expected to go up and down stairs on crutches. In 1963, at the age of nineteen, he under went the first of five operations in order to allow his muscles to develop and do away with his leg braces. Unfortunately, mistakes were made during one of the operations, and as a result a sixth operation had to be carried out in order to correct the problem.

The combined effect of all of these operations was the loss of most of his movement in the left hip as well as the loss of a full range of motion in his knees. This meant that when Zev fell, his legs did not bend the way a normal joint would, causing him extreme pain. This in turn led to his refusal to walk. The result was that he was confined to a wheelchair because his leg muscles were wasting away.

Zev decided to live on his own and came to Toronto in 1977. He lived in a private apartment for people with handicaps from 1979 to 1986, then in another similar apartment from 1986 to 2002.

Being in a wheelchair and living for the most part alone in a handicapped apartment became more and more difficult for Zev. An example was getting on and off the toilet on his own. Once he realized he was having difficulty, he decided it was time to move into a long-term care home, and he came to Lincoln Place Nursing Home in October 2002.

Zev wrote an article that was printed in the July 2006 edition of the *Town Crier Newspaper*. It says in part:

> Lincoln Place Nursing Home is located in the Forest Hill area of Toronto.

I have been living here since October 2002. I enjoy life here very much. There is an Orthodox Synagogue in the building where the full range of Jewish life takes place during the year.... Every month there is a birthday party where all the residents born during a particular month celebrate. All residents are invited.

There is a talk group where participants can express there. The psychiatrist runs the group.

I wish to mention my observation about the building itself. It is built in such a way that one cannot help but run into other people. This is really good because one does not feel lonely. I have been in other places where one can avoid bumping into people unless it is absolutely necessary.

In my view all nursing homes should be built in the manner of Lincoln Place.

In closing I would like to say that what matters to me most is global warming and the destruction of the environment as well as trying to understand the threat of terrorism. To this end I keep abreast of world events both political and scientific. I am a layman in these matters and as of the present I have no solution. However I am doing what I can by just trying to understand the complex problems.

In Lincoln Place, he receives the full range of care — everything from meals to showers to laundry. He was always afraid of burning himself in the kitchen when he prepared his own meals in his apartment. He receives assistance with dressing and bathing, yet he has his independence. He goes out to malls to see movies and goes shopping for such things as computers and other electronic items. He has several friends that he visits around Toronto. All this is done with the help of Wheel Trans. Zev loves the support that he receives to help him move around the community. He does not like having to sign in to and out of the home, but that is the only part of the process with which he is uncomfortable.

The reason Zev prefers Lincoln Place to the apartments available for people with disabilities is that he found the nurses in the other facilities avoided him, whereas at Lincoln Place he is a part of a community. He is close with both the other residents and the staff.

Zev's mother is living at the Baycrest Centre for Geriatric Care, and he visits her on a regular basis. The reason his mother lives at Baycrest and he lives at Lincoln Place is that both he and his mother felt it was important for Zev to be independent. He also used to travel by plane to see his brother and his family but is unable to do that now as he has less stamina as well as less mobility.

When asked about the negative aspects of aging, Zev said losing some of his teeth did not make him feel great. He also dislikes losing muscle mass and having his hair thin out and become gray. To counteract this, he lifts weights and goes to physiotherapy at Lincoln Place on a regular basis. He exercises his mind by reading a lot.

Zev said he has a strong will to live as he has been through so much, and now he is enjoying his life. He always wanted his life story told and now it is happening.

When asked about what matters to him he mentioned global warming and the destruction of the environment, as well as the threat of terrorism. He also feels people should not be too quick to judge others, as "we all have weaknesses."

Profile 10

~

EARL EDIAL JOSEPH ALBRECHT

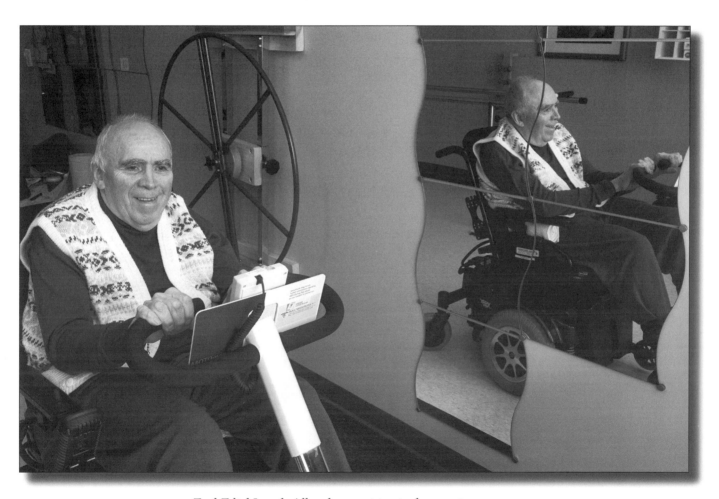

Earl Edial Joseph Albrecht exercising in the exercise room at
Leisureworld Caregiving Centre, Ellesmere, Scarborough, Ontario.

Earl Edial Joseph Albrecht

Minister, Ontario College of Art & Design graduate, husband, father, grandfather, and writer.

Born: Milverton, Ontario, Canada, 1935
Home: Leisureworld Caregiving Centre, Ellesmere, Scarborough, Ontario

ADJUST TO ACCOMMODATE CHANGE

"Often as people are aging they think a stroke or Alzheimer's disease does not happen to them. People need to make adjustments to accommodate these changes that happen in life. I hope my writing will help others who have disabilities and also help the younger generation. Young people need to have varied interests and should be more flexible and adapt to loss and change. All people should fill the vacuum in life with creativity."

I believe it is important to:

- "Have a mature belief in God"
- "Write and be creative"
- "Use a computer"
- "Accept who you are and your current situation"

March 2007

History: minister, Ontario College of Art and Design graduate, husband, father, grandfather, writer

Born: Milverton, Ontario, 1935

Currently resident at: Leisureworld Caregiving Centre — Ellesmere, Scarborough, Ontario

Keys to enjoying his later years: Accepting himself and his current situation; having a changing belief in God; writing; using a computer; applying his creativity

Why in a long-term care home: The need for assistance because of various infirmities; the freedom to pursue his interests; the opportunity to have his own room

~~

As a young boy in Milverton, Earl did well at school and always liked extracurricular activities, particularly those that appealed to his artistic nature. In high school, he especially enjoyed creating stage sets for the school's Gilbert and Sullivan operettas. His family consisted of his parents, Elie and Emma, and one sister, Shirley (now Shirley Schaeffer).

After completing Grade 13, Earl attended the Ontario College of Art and Design, where he majored in interior design. He got a job in London, Ontario, working in the display department at the Robert Simpson Company.

Several years later Earl decided to attend Huron College, where he enrolled in a pre-theology course for two years. Next he attended Waterloo Lutheran University (now Wilfrid Laurier University) and received his Bachelor of Arts and a Bachelor of Divinity. He became a Lutheran minister and was in the clergy for twenty-nine years.

Earl and his wife, Sandra, then moved to Fredericton, New Brunswick. Along with a few other people, Earl started a Gilbert and Sullivan Society, presenting one play a year; Earl was involved in sets and costumes. Sandra worked as a teacher, and they had two children, Elizabeth and Stephen.

Earl found his art studies very enriching, and he felt fortunate to weave together art and the ministry. The ministry allowed him to become involved with people and their lives, and the artistic side helped with his creativity and remained an abiding interest throughout his life.

Earl developed multiple sclerosis (MS) in his mid fifties. He and his wife purchased an old schoolhouse called the Pearl Lake School House, which was built in 1873. They were able to live in it for six years until Earl required more care. Earl said at times he felt useless and bitter because of his illness. Because of the MS, he was limited in what he could do. He began to write and was able to work through some of his negative feelings. The writing challenged him and proved to be excellent therapy.

His writing, which he still pursues, deals with handicapped seniors and his growing skepticism for religion. His writing also helps him with his computer skills, and he has now completed three books. He says that the computer is his saving grace.

When Earl was on a disability pension, he was unable to work as a minister, but when he reached sixty-five and received his Old Age Security pension, he could once again be a minister as he was classified as retired, not disabled.

When Earl moved to Leisureworld Caregiving Centre — Ellesmere in 2003, he was one of the first residents there and began to lead religious services. Earl is visited by his wife, his children, and his grandchildren on a regular basis. He takes Wheel Trans to family barbeques in the summer and attends other celebrations throughout the year. He also attends various group outings that are arranged for the residents at Leisureworld.

Earl is a quiet person and finds that having his own room at Leisureworld allows him to think and write. His writing helps him resolve his own situation, and if his books are one day published he hopes they will help others as well. He is also writing a history of the schoolhouse that the family bought and still uses. Earl usually visits the schoolhouse every summer with his wife and their children and grandchildren.

Earl does not want to live long enough to become very weak. He explains that he will be satisfied when his time is up, and he is at peace with himself. When Earl reflects on how his life has changed over the years, he finds that he has matured in his religion, becoming more cynical. He sometimes doubts the existence of a God as he asks himself why there is so much pain and suffering in the world. Although he does not have an answer for the question yet, he is working on finding one.

Earl left me with a thought. He said that a person may have to say farewell to one situation and hello to a new and better situation.

Following is an excerpt from Earl's writings:

"I want to go home. I hate this place."

Such sentiments may distress a spouse, family, and friends. Negativity is disturbing. Staff at long-term care facilities are able to help residents and families.

Being a resident in a long-term care facility permits me to speak from personal experience. It provides insights gleaned from fellow residents and my own, as we come to terms with living in a long-term care community.

Unwillingness to adapt to change causes serious problems and avoidable pain. Is the resident being unreasonable, selfish? Has the person always been like this?

Lifestyles change; disability, age, and other circumstances often require radical changes. We may be angry about what has happened to us, deny its impact on us, and resent changes forced on us. We have always been in control, able to do what we want when we want. Letting go is difficult. Requiring and getting assistance may be intolerable, restrictions and limitations offensive.

There may be no alternative for what is required. Guardians and families must make difficult and sometimes unpopular decisions. Anger is common. All feel helpless and terrible. The resident feels helpless and terrible.

How prepared are any of us for radical change?

Change is inevitable. We do our families and ourselves a favour by preparing for change. Flexibility is important. Accepting the view that there are other ways of preparing food than the way we always did it is elemental. Residents must eat. Routines we considered inviolable may suddenly have to be altered. There are many things we used to do that we are no longer able to do. We may refuse to accept that fact. The assistance of others becomes necessary, and hopefully appreciated.

Guidance counsellors assist in making career choices. Plans in which we invest help us in many ways. Preparing for retirement is wise and so is preparing for change.

Illness, disability, age, and tragedy radically change lives. We don't want to dwell on these topics, but unfortunately they happen. Preparing for these possibilities is wise.

Writing is therapeutic for me. There are many stories in residents' lives; examples of adversity overcome, a long life lived, adapting to disability, heroism, successes, accomplishments, and failures. These stories may become the nucleus for ideas yet to be developed.

Attitude is important. "I always did it this way, the only way!" shuts doors to experiencing other ways. This attitude can become a noose. We prepare for change by being tolerant, adaptable, and flexible when we are young and healthy.

Past can present us with a triptych of rich memories not to broadcast, boast, and bore, but to savour, perhaps in the confines of a wheelchair or bed. Present can be flooded with possibilities. When there is a willingness to change, develop new interests, attempt untried challenges, we help ourselves and others. Being prepared to give up former ways and interests, being excited by the new and unfamiliar ways and interests, also helps. "I never tried that before" is a helpful, hopeful attitude.

Not everyone is overwhelmed by change. Many adjust to long-term care without any problems. Experiencing new situations and facing unfamiliar challenges can be exciting. Things we used to do, but are no longer able to do, may be discouraging and leave us feeling depressed. They can also be prods moving us in totally unexpected directions. "I didn't think I could do that" becomes a positive statement of growth and accomplishment.

Adapting to the unfamiliar can be invigorating, change a positive life force.

"I like it here. This is my home. Thank you."

Profile 11

⁓

ROBERT E. AND JOSEPHINE ELIZABETH RANSOM

Beth and Bob Ransom in the solarium at The Westbury, Etobicoke, Ontario.

Robert (Bob) E. Ransom

Teamster, army veteran, insurance sales representative, volunteer, husband, father, grandfather, great-grandfather.

Born: Toronto, Ontario, Canada, 1925
Home: The Westbury, Etobicoke, Ontario

Josephine (Beth) Ransom

Product demonstrator, public liaison for large shopping centre, wife, mother, grandmother, great-grandmother.

Born: Vandeleur, Ontario, Canada, 1926
Home: The Westbury, Etobicoke

FOCUS ON THE LIGHT

"We find that our health has actually improved since we moved into the Westbury as the care we require is right at hand. We work out in the 'Exercise & Wellness Room' and also by walking outside. It is like having a second chance at life! The wisdom we offer to people younger than ourselves is to be happy. Focus on the light and not the darkness."

We believe it is important to:

- "Enjoy family and each other"
- "Believe in God and be spiritual"
- "Participate in programs at the nursing home"
- "Continue in leadership roles to be a voice for residents."

March 2007

History: Bob: Teamster, dairy farm worker, veteran, insurance representative, district commissioner for the Boy Scouts of Canada, husband, father, grandfather, great-grandfather; Beth: Factory worker, product demonstrator, liaison for large shopping centre, volunteer, wife, mother, grandmother, great-grandmother

Born: Bob: Toronto, Ontario, 1925; Beth: Vandeleur, Ontario, 1926

Keys to enjoying their later years: Volunteering; being concerned about others; enjoying family and each other; believing in God; being spiritual; adapting to change and loss

Why in a long-term care home: Receiving physical, medical, and emotional support from the staff; participating in programs at the long-term care home; voicing the concerns of residents

Robert Ransom, known as Bob, attended Oriole Park Public School and Northern Vocational High School in Toronto. When Bob left high school he went to work on a dairy farm in Inniskillin, Ontario. He was hired on as a teamster, and his responsibility was to maintain the horses.

Josephine Elizabeth, known as Beth, had four brothers (Frank, Raymond, who died young, Mort, and Ted) and one sister (Pat); she is the second oldest. She went to Vandeleur Public School, a one-room schoolhouse with one teacher for all subjects. After finishing school, she worked at Victory Aircraft, later known as A.V. Roe, at the Malton Airport.

Bob's next job was in Nestleton, Ontario, where he once again helped maintain horses and did general farm work. As the Second World War loomed, he joined the army and was a private from 1943 to 1945, serving in Canada.

After his army service, Bob went to Alberta during harvest time and worked there for a short while before leaving to go back to the farm in Nestleton. In 1947, after learning that his mother, Ruth, had been killed by a drunk driver, Bob decided to move back to Toronto to be with his father, Horace. Horace was the owner, president, and CEO of Ribbons Ltd., which merchandized ribbons that were used in making hats and dresses, wrapping gift, hemming skirts, and various other purposes.

Bob was hired on by the T. Eaton Co. to do clerical work He met Beth while working at Eaton's. She was a demonstrator for the kitchen equipment company Silex.

They were married in 1949. When they met it was love at first sight, and they still enjoy each other's company. After getting married they moved to Edmonton and lived there until 1955. Bob worked for the London Life Insurance Company as an agent, and Beth was busy with their three children, Ruth, Kim, and Pam.

Both Bob and Beth have been committed to being active volunteers over the years. While the children were growing up, Beth volunteered at their school and was involved in the Girl Guides. Bob was a member of the Masonic Order and served on several committees with the Grey Bruce District Health Council in Owen Sound and with the Wiarton Hospital; he had also served as the District Commissioner for the Boy Scouts of Canada while living in Toronto. Bob and Beth have also been members of the Royal Canadian Legion; Bob is a lifetime member.

After they moved back to Toronto again, a fourth child, Wendy, was born. Bob got a job working for All-state Insurance Company and worked there for more than thirty years. When the children were old enough, Beth went to work at the Yorkdale Shopping Centre. She was the only person at the information desk, and she often worked with the fire, police, and maintenance departments. The job was challenging and rewarding. She worked there until both she and Bob retired in 1986. They were in their early sixties.

Bob and Beth had always wanted to purchase a piece of property outside of the city, and they found their dream home in Hepworth, Ontario, on thirty-six acres of land surrounded by a forest. There was also a stunning large garden and beautiful ponds. They lived there for eighteen years. Bob loved to hunt and fish, and Beth would prepare wonderful picnics for the family to enjoy together. They also enjoyed going out in the boat together.

The couple especially loved to dance and sing. This passion was one of the greatest pleasures in their marriage. Bob played at long-term care homes and at the Royal Canadian Legion in Wiarton, Branch 208. On Wednesday afternoons they hosted a jamboree. Bob was the master of ceremonies and Beth was the hostess. There were twenty to thirty musicians who met weekly at this wonderful event. Bob played the ukelele banjo and sang. They brought a tremendous amount of joy and happiness to people for nine years.

While living in Hepworth, Beth developed rheumatoid arthritis, and gradually her health deteriorated. They went to a hospital in Wiarton for her treatment at the same time that Bob had two hip operations. They were both reluctant to move into a long-term care home, but life was too difficult to cope with in Hepworth.

When they began to think of a long-term care home, there was a lack of accommodation that they liked up north, so Bob and Beth decided to sell their home and move back to Toronto to be closer to their children. The Community Care Access Centre did the initial investigation, and they recommended that the couple should move into a long-term care residence for safety and support.

They moved into The Westbury in Toronto in 2004 at its opening, going from owning a large piece of property to living in one large room. When asked about how they adapted to these changes, they said that it is what you make of it. You can focus on either the negative or the positive.

Beth was brought to The Westbury on a stretcher and was told that she would never walk again. But her health soon improved with the home's excellent care. She feels that her second chance at life is due to medication, determination, Bob's assistance, and her own motivation.

Bob and Beth are both committed to making The Westbury the number one home in long-term care in Ontario. They are passionate about the recreation programs and having a consistent staff that care for and are knowledgeable about the residents. They encourage the staff to treat the residents as adults, not children. They enjoy rallying the residents together so that they have a united voice, and they ensure that everyone has an opportunity to voice their questions, concerns, and recommendations. With the support and leadership of Bob and Beth, The Westbury will certainly be moving in a positive direction for years to come.

They are very comfortable with the overall environment. Beth walks with a walker, and she now is able to walk miles both inside and outside. Her arthritis has been stabilized and she is mobile again. They are in the exercise and wellness room on their floor several days a week.

The director of the home, Nelson Ribeiro, asked Bob in 2005 if he would like to be the president of the Residents' Council, and Bob is now in his third term. As president, Bob deals with general concerns, complaints, and criticisms of residents. Bob brings the issues to the executive board for recommendation and administration.

When it comes to their current living arrangements, Beth adjusted quickly, and Bob is still adjusting. Both say that attitude is everything in getting used to life in a long-term care home. As Beth said, "This is my home, and I'll do whatever I can to make it as enjoyable as possible."

Bob and Beth go to most of the events and activities at The Westbury, including cards, art classes, shuffleboard, movies, pub nights, bingo, and sometimes singing to other residents.

Both Bob and Beth feel that God has given them the strength to carry on. They said their reason for living is for each other. They feel religion and spirituality has played a major role for them throughout their lives.

The wisdom they offer to younger people is to smile, sing, dance, be involved in each other's lives, and have an optimistic outlook. A person is known by the company he keeps. They think it is harder for young people today as there are so many choices and too many temptations.

What matters to them is family, including their three daughters, a son, three grandchildren, and one great-granddaughter, as well as each other, God, maintaining optimum health, and adapting to change and loss. Bob says he strives to better the lives of others.

Profile 11

~

ANDREW ROBERTS

Andrew Roberts writing in his room at Bethany Lodge, Unionville, Ontario.

Andrew Roberts

Marine engineer, clerical worker, husband, father, participant in church activities, writer since age 98.

Born: Liverpool, England, United Kingdom, 1902
Home: Bethany Lodge, Unionville, Ontario

HOW OLD IS "OLD"?

When I was less than 10 years of age,
And saw the "old" people of 20 going out for an evening
And staying out until 10 p.m.
I thought it must be nice to be "old" like that.
And not have to go to bed at 8:30.
At age 20, like the words of the song,
"I've got the key of the door, never been 21 before."
I can stay out real late….
Well, in a few months, (D.V.), I'll be 100 years old, and I don't see any "old" folks I can envy
But I look back over the years.
Yes, there were some happy events, and some sad, but the PRESENT is mine!
The Lord has been good to me, and He will keep me to the end.
And, when one day I say goodbye to this sad old world,
Who can say, how old is "old"?

Excerpted from a poem written by Andrew Roberts that won 1st place at the Markham Fair, 2002.

March 2007

History: Marine engineer, clerical worker, husband, father, participant in church activities, writer since age ninety-eight

Born: Liverpool, England, 1902

Currently resident at: Bethany Lodge, Unionville, Ontario

Keys to enjoying his later years: Believing in God; making friends with younger people; adapting to the changing circumstances to life; being part of a community; applying his creativity to his writing

Why in a long-term care home: The need for assistance because of various infirmities; the freedom to pursue his interests; friendship with other residents in being part of a community; opportunities provided for religious services and pastimes

‿

Andrew attended Walton National Church of England School until Grade 8. He came from a family of six children born to Henry and Agnes Roberts. The youngest, Edward, died at age six, leaving Andrew two brothers, William and Frederick, and two sisters, Margaret and Magdalene.

Andrew had a happy boyhood, and his memories are of bicycles, roller skates, cats, dogs, and a parrot. He often went to Bedford Hall, the cinema across from his school, which played silent films. Andrew was always athletic: he was involved with an English cricket club in the summer months and cross-country running in the winter months.

Following Grade 8, Andrew apprenticed for five years to become a marine engineer. He graduated at twenty-one but was not able to find any work in that area in England, so he moved to Hamilton, Ontario, in 1927. He ended up working for Procter and Gamble for forty years doing clerical work.

He married Jessie in 1932. They had met in England, and she followed him to Canada.

They bought their first house in Hamilton in 1940 for $2,600. They had one son, Donald Andrew. Donald married Catherine, and they have two children, Melissa and James Andrew.

Andrew would visit the elderly and the ill, as he and Jessie were very active in doing church work; they made many friends there.

After the children were grown and living on their own, Andrew and Jessie moved to Bethany Lodge in 1996 as Jessie was quite ill. After Jessie's death, Andrew began to write stories, something he had never done before. His writing career actually started at the age of ninety-eight.

The following is a poem written by Andrew that was the first-place winner at the Markham Fair in 2002:

> When I was less than 10 years of age,
> And saw the "old" people of 20 going
>   out for an evening
> And staying out until 10 p.m.
> I thought it must be nice to be "old" like
>   that.
> And not have to go to bed at 8:30.

At age 20, like the words of the song,
"I've got the key of the door, never
been 21 before."
I can stay out real late.
But now, the "be home before 10 o'clock
or else"
Made me look at those "old" people of 40
who don't have to ask their mothers
for money
To go to the show or other places.
It must be nice to be that old, and
working, and have money to spend.
Wait until I'm that old.
At 40 years of age, I used to look at the
"old" people of 60, talking about
retirement and trips.
Just imagine, how lucky to be that old,
and not have to go out to work every day.
When 60 came and retirement, family
ties curtailed the travelling.
But I saw those "old" people of 80 going
on a cruise.
I looked forward to being that old with
my family married, so I'd be able to
go places.
Then, when 80 came, I'd see those "old"
people of 100, having a good time,
sitting in their chairs
And saying, "when I was young…"
They had other people to look after
them and had no worries, just taking things easy.
Maybe when I get that old.

Well, in a few months, (D.V.), I'll be
100 years old, and I don't see any
"old" folks I can envy
But I look back over the years.
Yes, there were some happy events,
and some sad, but the PRESENT
is mine!
The Lord has been good to me, and He
will keep me to the end.
And, when one day I say goodbye to
this sad old world,
Who can say, how old is "old"?

Andrew likes the people who live in the long-term care home. He has made several friendships that would not have developed if he lived alone at home. He feels that he is part of a community. He said it is important to be flexible when adapting to a changing situation in your life.

He has a machine in his room to help him exercise his legs, and he also walks. For his mind he does crossword puzzles and Sudoku. He watches movies that are provided at the long-term care home, reads, and goes to the Gospel Hall located across from his residence (it is called the Christian Brethren and is Protestant).

Andrew feels satisfied with his life and is proud of being 104 years old. His mind is clear, and he is thankful to God for this. Andrew's advice for others is: don't smoke; don't drink or take drugs; don't eat pickles; eat chocolates; go to church, keep breathing; and exercise.

Most of Andrew's friends have died, so he has made friends with a younger family and their children. He still feels wanted as younger people like him.

Profile 13

~

MAUREEN HUTCHINSON

Maureen Hutchinson has an office of her own at West Park Long Term Care Centre, Toronto.

Maureen Hutchinson

Librarian, university graduate, President of Ontario Association of Residents' Councils (OARC), fundraiser, mother.

Born: Dublin Ireland, 1920
Home: West Park Long Term Care Centre, Toronto

LIVE IN THE PRESENT

"Life is a continuous learning process until the moment we draw our last breath. We must relish the changes at each stage of our lives. In our youth we are eager recipients of knowledge: as we grow older we can enjoy the rewarding experience of learning new ideas and sharing our past with others in the community. Remember, it is not the years in your life that count; it is the life in your years. Live in the present, the past is gone; the future is not here and if we squander time in the present we are out of touch with life. Keep active, alert, alive, and keep growing!"

I believe it is important to:

- "Respect one another. Be tolerant of others' cultures and lifestyles"
- "Be generous. Show compassion for those less fortunate"
- "Safeguard the environment"
- "Provide better health resources to control wide spread diseases and to deal with epidemics"

March 2007

History: Librarian, university graduate, spokesperson for seniors, fundraiser, mother

Born: Dublin, Ireland, 1920

Currently resident in: West Park Long Term Care Centre, Toronto, Ontario

Keys to enjoying her later years: continuing to learn; relishing change; helping others by speaking and fundraising for them as president of the Resident's Council at West Park and president of the Ontario Association of Residents' Councils (OARC); sharing her past with others; keeping active, alert, and alive

Why in a long-term care home: Enjoying the grounds and gardens; getting involved with the Residents' Council and advocating for seniors in other long-term residences; having a private room

_⇜_

Maureen was born in Dublin, Ireland. Her parents were David and Sydney Ann Davidson. She did have a brother, James, who has since died. Her father was employed by Guinness Brewery, and her mother was a homemaker.

Maureen attended St. Columba's Public School and St. Mary's High School. Both of the schools were run by the Holy Faith Homes Catholic School Organization.

Outside of school, she was involved in learning to cook, taking art classes, and exercising. She also took some singing lessons, but she said that she could not sing

and was "thrown out." She had a happy childhood, and although the family was small she had many cousins, aunts, and uncles. All of her grandparents were deceased.

Maureen spent two years at university to study to become a librarian. She has a diploma in librarianship from University College in Dublin, which was part of the National University of Ireland.

Maureen met her husband, Aidan Hutchinson, in Dublin and they were married in 1952. She had worked as a librarian in the Dublin Public Library system until her marriage. In those days females had to retire upon marriage, but Maureen managed to bend the rules a little. Maureen did stop working when she became pregnant with their son, Kenneth, who was born and died in 1953. After their son died, she worked as manager of the library section of a bookshop in Dublin until 1955, when she and her husband moved to Canada where she began to work again in a library department in a bookstore.

Maureen and Aidan lived in Ajax, Ontario, for a year, where she was in charge of a library. Her husband worked in the Ministry of the Attorney General as an assistant court registrar. Maureen then began working at the University of Toronto as a librarian at- Sigmund Samuel Library in the King's College Circle. Maureen worked in the humanities section until she got pregnant again.

She stopped working while their son, Paul Joseph, was young. Then she went back to work part-time for a few months and then full-time until she retired in 1985. She worked her way up to deputy chief librarian of the Robarts Library, although she spent one year as acting chief after her retirement.

Maureen and Aidan moved into a retirement home in 1996 due to Aidan's declining health and lived there for four years until 2000, when they were both in their seventies. At that point Maureen and Aidan moved to Lincoln Place Nursing Home where they lived there together until Aidan passed away in December 2001. Maureen did not stay at Lincoln Place as she wanted a private room, so she moved to the West Park facility, which was also close to family.

When asked what we all can do to make the world a better place to live in Maureen responded by saying, "Respect one another. Be tolerant of others' cultures and lifestyles. Be generous. Show compassion for those less fortunate. Safeguard the environment. Provide better health resources to control wide spread diseases and to deal with epidemics."

Maureen does not worry as much as she grows older. At this stage of life one has already been through so much that facing the challenges that life presents becomes easier. She is resigned to life's challenges.

Maureen is president of the Residents' Council at West Park and is also president of the Ontario Association of Residents' Councils and a member of the Senior Advisory Panel of the Toronto Central Local Health Integrated Network. In March 2007 she wrote the following piece about the work that she is doing.

THE FLIGHT OF TIME: A 5-YEAR SAGA

March 7, 2007, marked the fifth anniversary of my residency in West Park Long Term Care Centre. I find it hard to realize that so much time has passed and so quickly: there just never seem to be enough hours in the day for everything. This was not how I imagined my future on that March day in 2002. I was eighty-two years old, recently widowed, with no family or household responsibilities and in reasonably good health. I could foresee a delightfully pleasant and indolent life enjoying the sun in the beautiful courtyards, walking through the magnificent grounds, communing with nature. Oh, boy, how wrong I was!

When I retired in 1985 I vowed never again to serve on a committee, attend a meeting, negotiate resolutions, write a report, conduct a survey, etc.; so what was the first thing I did soon after my arrival? I can't believe that I was (very easily, I must admit) persuaded to run for presidency of the Residents' Council being formed in May. Of course nobody else was foolish enough to express interest then or in succeeding years so I am still the figurehead, at least until 2008.

I quickly learned that fundraising (to assist in provision of activities for all residents) was an essential responsibility of Council and that I had to organize Summer and Christmas Raffles each year and that the first raffle would be in July! Fortunately a resident donated a beautiful handmade afghan and the raffle was a great success with proceeds of more than $1300 for just the one prize. In the years since that first effort I have organized a total of ten raffles which have involved solicitation of many prizes and have produced a regular source of funds used for the benefit of all residents. Other funds for Council have been raised through Book Sales and White Elephant Sales, once or twice yearly depending on the quantities of donated goods. Additionally fundraising has been done for Community Outreach Programs such as Daily Bread Bank, Heart and Stroke Foundation, Alzheimer's Society, Canadian Cancer Society, [and] Adopt-a-family for Christmas. Residents' Council also did fundraising for such tragedies as [the] tsunami and [Hurricane] Katrina.

In other words everything grew like Topsy! Hallelujah for all the residents and staff and family members who helped me so much.

All of this involvement should have been enough for me, but I am a devil for punishment so there I went again. The first issue of WPLTCC Newsletter was produced in June 2002 and was edited by Zoie. Somehow, and I can't remember very clearly, I became the editor of the [Autumn] issue and continue to write, edit, and produce four issues [under the title *Tidings*] each year. I don't know whether this changeover a was a result of crafty manipulation by Zoie or due to overeagerness on my part to get a chance to write something other than the factual reports that were so much a necessity during my years in academia. Whatever the reason, I have never regretted taking on this task: it is my favourite occupation. I just wish I had more time to devote to it.

Summer 2003 was a turning point for me! A computer was donated for residents' use; recreation department offered computer lessons; I took three or four lessons and was completely hooked. Six months later I bought my own computer and the rest for me is history! I am a devotee of the Internet, a daily e-mail correspondent, [and] a constant user of word processing for minutes, memos newsletters, signs, etc. I have even progressed (slowly) to use of clip-art for illustration. And all this for someone who never even learned to type! Stores like Staples and Office Depot are now among my favourite shopping spots and it is quite exciting to order items on-line and to have them arrive the next day. I never would have believed that there were so many varieties and weights of paper or that choosing a design paper could be as thrilling as selecting a new dress. Ordering from book suppliers like Amazon is efficient but lacks the pure joy experienced browsing in bookstores like Book Mark or Book City on Bloor West so there I continue to be a personal shopper. The computer changed my life but not my reading habits.

2004 was the first year WPLTCC was involved in the Accreditation Process. It was a very intensive time of self-examination and comparison with established standards in other homes. The achievement award — Certified Accreditation for the three-year period 2004–2007 — was a well-earned and successful outcome. As President of Residents' Council I was a member of the team and found it to be an interesting and informative experience. The 2007 team (of which I am also a member) has now started work in preparation for the Accreditation review in November 2007.

In the same year, on Zoie's recommendation, I applied for and was accepted as a member of the Executive Board of OARC [Ontario Association of Residents' Councils]. I quickly became very involved in related operations; I was asked to be the OARC representative on the Consumer Panel to review the public website being set up by MOHLTC [Ministry of Health and Long-Term Care] to provide easily accessible and up-to-date information about all Long-Term Care Homes in Ontario. Later I was invited to join the Executive Director of OARC on the Standards Review Group which was working with the MOHLTC Director of Care on the review of all standards for LTC homes. This again was a great learning experience as other members were from various organizations concerned with the care and rights of seniors but I was the only resident. As an executive member of OARC I attended a meeting with Monique Smith and legal staff with regard to the new MOH standards.

In 2005, on the home front, I took over responsibility for the operation [for a limited number of hours per week] of a small Café and Gift Shop. This provides a useful and popular service especially for family visitors and is manned by resident volunteers. Supplies are purchased out of revenue and the operations are self-sustaining.

Also in 2005 a Family Council was established in WPLTCC. As Residents' Council President I have been involved in a liaison capacity and have found the connection very useful. I and another member of our executive attend the monthly meetings and have a great deal of input on behalf of the residents.

In June 2006 I was elected President of OARC with a consequent increase in responsibilities and more attendance at meetings with the ministry, workshops, [and] other organizations with concerns for seniors. Such activities included:

- WPLTCC was asked by OARC to participate in its 25th anniversary project "Working with your Residents' Council" by being the cover girls on the information binder and CD (I and two members of the Residents' Council Executive and Zoie Mohammed, Programs Manager). The binder was distributed in December 2006 to 600+ homes in Ontario and has been enthusiastically received.
- In September I and the Executive Director of OARC met with Minister George Smitherman and Monique Smith to discuss Bill 140 and were invited with some others to Queen's Park to attend the introduction of the bill and were welcomed into the legislature.
- The Executive Director and I were invited to a luncheon in honour of OARC's 25th anniversary.
- We were also invited with other interested groups to a Fact Finding

session in MOHLTC on Bill 140.
- In November I attended an all-day workshop at the Wellesley Institute on "Board Governance for Non-Profit Organizations."
- The Executive Director and I were invited to a luncheon with two Executive Members of OLTCA to discuss Bill 140.
- The Executive Director and I attended an MOH all-day meeting to discuss the goal of developing a ten-year health system strategic plan and participated in a Stake Holders' Roundtable Discussion.

As my responsibilities, both in-house and externally, have increased so has the amount of paperwork grown to mountainous proportions, and this in what is supposed to be "the paperless society"! I have pack rat tendencies, which worsen the situation further. As my bedroom became a disaster area I lobbied management successfully for an office; end result two paper-cluttered rooms!

Profile 14

≈

EDWARD SIMAN

Eddie Siman is using a board to point to letters — this is how he communicates.
He is surrounded by his children at The Village of Erin Meadows, Mississauga, Ontario.

Edward (Eddie) Siman

Woodworker, milk deliveryman, electrician, entrepreneur, father, grandfather.

Born: Toronto, Ontario, Canada, 1934
Home: The Village of Erin Meadows, Mississauga, Ontario

THE NEED TO HAVE HIS VOICE HEARD

"Although I am unable to speak due to Parkinson's disease, I communicate by using a board with letters on it and a pointer to make my immediate thoughts known. I am still alive and want to be heard very much. I use a keyboard and a computer so my bigger and detailed messages are communicated. The main message I want to share with others is that the world would be a better place to live in if we all stopped the fighting and the wars."

I believe it is important to:

- "Maintain a positive attitude to life"
- "Continue to do hobbies such as woodworking"
- "Be open to receiving family and other support"
- "Strongly believe in God and be active in your church"
- "Always stay involved"
- "Socialize and exercise with others"

March 2007

History: Woodworker, milk-deliveryman, electrician, entrepreneur, father, grandfather

Born: Toronto, Ontario, 1934

Currently resident at: The Village of Erin Meadows, Mississauga

Keys to enjoying his later years: Having a positive attitude to life; exercising; continuing his passion for woodworking; believing in God; being involved with the lives of his children and grandchildren; seeing old friends and making new friends

Why in a long-term care home: Proximity to previous residence and family; need for assistance as a result of various infirmities arising from Parkinson's (especially the inability to verbally communicate); social activities and interaction with other residents

Edward Siman went to public school in Toronto. His parents, Maria and Ferdinand, had two other children, Jerry and Emil, who died at the age of one. When Eddie was twelve, the family returned to their native Slovakia for eighteen months but came back to Canada.

When Eddie returned from Slovakia, he was able to speak English and Slovak. His first job was at age fourteen, doing electrical work (rewinding motors) in a factory. After that job, he delivered milk for Silverwoods Dairy, where he was the top salesman for five years.

Then he was involved in a business that sold safety shoes. He did that for thirty-five years, and he was very satisfied with his work.

Eddie met his wife, Mary, in 1952 at a church dance in their neighbourhood of Dundas and Roncesvalles, and they were married in 1954. They had two sons, Ron and Jim. They now have two daughters-in-laws and three grandchildren.

Eddie retired at age sixty-three, as he had been diagnosed with Parkinson's disease in his mid to late fifties.

Mary died in 2003. She suffered from kidney problems, and had had a kidney transplant and a knee replacement. Mary and Eddie were still living in their home when Mary passed away, although they did have some services from a home support agency to help with Mary's care. Eddie lived on his own with supports for a year but then moved to The Village of Erin Meadows, a Mississauga long-term care home. The need became obvious when the family went on a holiday together; when they were with Eddie for twenty-four hours a day they saw how much difficulty he was having trying to manage on his own, and they realized that he needed more care.

Mary had checked out the long-term care home prior to her death, and the family chose The Village of Erin Meadows because it was close to the family and felt like a community.

The family found the long-term care home to be progressive. There is an atrium with gardening facilities, an arts and crafts centre, and a dining area where friends can join for a meal. The staff is genuinely supportive and helpful; there are residents and volunteers of all ages. The family feels that the staff is passionate about what they do.

There are fundraising events, and Eddie sells some of the woodwork that he does. He donates the proceeds to the Parkinson's Society. In the summer the facility has events outside on the lawn. Grandchildren, families, and friends are involved.

Eddie started his passion for woodworking while he was living at home, where he had a workshop area. In the long-term care home the wood is cut for him because it is too difficult for him to do himself due to his Parkinson's. The facility is concerned about the safety of the residents near the odours from the paints that he is using, and the facility may build another area where paint can be used.

Eddie lost his ability to communicate verbally over the last two years. Now he uses both a computer and a card with letters and a pointer to communicate.

He has found meaning in life by doing his woodworking, being involved with the lives of his children and grandchildren, seeing old friends, and making new friends. He also enjoys going to social activities and interacting with other residents. He participates in exercise classes (and sometimes he leads the class!).

Eddie has always been a positive person. For him the glass was always half full. Eddie's son Jim feels that his father has always had a positive attitude partly because of the fact that his mother was at home when he was young. He had a good experience in his work life: he got along very well with his boss, and he found meaning in the work that he did. He also had a loving wife and two loving sons.

Having a strong belief in God and being active in the church has helped Eddie throughout his life, especially now with his inability to communicate verbally. His strong faith has helped him. His loving and supportive family is very important to Eddie.

Profile 15

VERNON McCUTCHEON

Specialty Care Bradford Valley Program,
Intergenerational reading St. Jean de Brebeuf

An intergenerational reading program is operated out of St. Jean de Brebeuf School in Bradford, Ontario.
Student Alexa Paulos (left) sits beside Vernon McCutcheon (centre), as he reads to her.
Kathy Wheeler (right) is the social worker from Specialty Care Bradford.

Intergenerational Reading Program

Operated jointly between St. Jean de Brebeuf School, Bradford and Specialty Care Bradford Valley.

Vernon McCutcheon

"This has been a learning experience for me. I look forward to going to St. Jean de Brebeuf School and reading to the children. They are very kind to me. When I was sick they sent me pictures that I showed to my family. Coming here takes me back — my children are in their 50's and my grandchildren at in their 20's. My oldest grandson teaches at Newmarket High School. I always gave my grandchildren books so they would learn there are no short cuts. I think these children are just as respectful as we were 75 years ago.

"The little ones will hug me and say they're glad I'm back. I think they're special. I'm a retired Ontario Land Surveyor; I know the whole province and I've seen a lot of changes. I used to go down the highway with a 100 foot tape; they don't do that any more. I look forward to these visits. I've always been an early riser; I wake up at 5:30 or 6 in the morning."

Kathy Wheeler

"Starting this project has been a lot of fun and an easy process to start as my three children (Hailee in JK, Jacob in grade 3 and Mackenzie in Grade 7) attend this school. All of the teachers and Mrs. Allen, the principal, are very supportive. The seniors love it because they know they are making a difference in the lives of so many. Each time they leave the school they rave about their extremely positive experience. It makes their day coming here. Mrs. Townsend has got other teachers involved so we have several classrooms for each visit. My daughter Hailee loves when Frank Macaluso comes to visit her classroom. He's her special friend and she's proud that he comes to her school. Jeannine Furze, who works in Restorative Care, comes so I have extra support from Specialty Care staff, too."

Alexa Paulos

"I like it when Vern comes to our classroom. Sometimes we read stories to him and show pictures. Vern tells us happy stories. I have one brother Christopher — he's 4 and going to kindergarten. I have two grandmas and two grandfathers. My grandpa is old: he's 47 or maybe he's 67."

March 2007

The intergenerational reading program was initiated by Karen Townsend, a Grade 2 teacher at St. Jean de Brebeuf, and Kathy Wheeler, Director of Resident and Family Services at Specialty Care Bradford Valley, a nearby long-term care facility, with the active support of Mrs. Allen, principal of this kindergarten to Grade 8 separate school. The program is operated jointly between St. Jean de Brebeuf School in Bradford and Specialty Care Bradford Valley.

Vernon McCutcheon said he will be eighty in three months (at the time of the interview in 2007). He said, "This has been a learning experience for me. The children are very kind. When I was sick they sent me pictures that I showed to my family. Coming here takes me back; my children are in their fifties and my grandchildren are in their twenties. My oldest grandson teaches at Newmarket High School. I always gave my grandchildren books so they would learn there are no shortcuts. I think these children are just as respectful as we were seventy-five years ago."

Frank Macaluso, age eighty-six, comments, "I have a lot of grandchildren, and I'm a great-grandfather too; I don't know where the time went. Some of my grandchildren are in Newmarket, and the ones in California phone me up but I don't see them very much. The kids here are very nice, and I like hearing them read. I worked at Canadian Tire at Yonge and Steeles in Toronto for twenty-five years. I was in charge of hardware: sinks, bathtubs, tools. I liked it there.

"I hope life will be better for these children; at this school they learn about Jesus before they are teenagers.

These days both parents have to work so the kids need lots of extra adult friends. Today I read three books to three different children. When they want me I'll come running. Hailie [Kathy Wheeler's daughter] is my special friend. She says 'Hullo, Frankie' every time she sees me.

"I have a lot to be thankful for. I don't refuse exercise, that way I can keep going even though I use this walker now."

Kathy Wheeler is the social worker at Specialty Care Bradford Valley. "Starting this project has been a lot of fun and an easy process to start as my three children (Hailee in JK, Jacob in grade 3 and Mackenzie in Grade 7) attend this school," she said. Jean Dube, age forty-seven, Karen Townsend's teaching assistant, said, "Seniors should be in every school; the children and the seniors both benefit. Children are learning to be storytellers, and seniors are storytellers already. In the Asian culture, children live with their elders, seniors are honoured and familiar. With this program, some of that same connection can happen."

Students enjoy the program as well. Alexa Paulos, age seven, said, "I like it when Vern comes to our classroom." Taylor Running said, "It's really fun having them visit us. I tell Vern different stories and I read to him. My sister, Summer, is three, she'll be four in August. My grandpas both died and my grandmas live far away, so I only see them on trips. That's really all I can tell you, that it's fun and I like it a lot when the visitors come to see us and help us read."

Profile 16

ELEANOR
MARY
RUSSELL

*Photo of Eleanor Russell is on the piano
at the family farm in Arcona, Ontario —
she had already passed away when the
photo was taken.*

Eleanor M. (Ellis) Russell

Amateur composer, musician, writer, poet, farmer's wife, volunteer in community and church, biblical student, wife, mother, grandmother.

Born: London, Ontario, Canada, 1913
Home: Specialty Care Mississauga Road to 2007

GROWING OLD ... A BLESSING

"Her strong Christian values guided her through her life. She always knew that God was in control of her life and it was He who would decide how her life would turn out. If, before bed, you would say to her, 'See you in the morning!' her reply was always 'God willing.' Growing old was not an expectation, it was a blessing. And dying was not something to be feared."

Heather Johnson, granddaughter

Mom believed it is important to:

- "Have a strong belief in God"
- "Look for the good in people"
- "Make life better for others"
- "Embrace life with enthusiasm"

Wendy Johnson, daughter

January 2007

History: amateur composer, musician, writer and poet, farmer's wife, volunteer, Bible student, wife, mother, grandmother

Born: London, Ontario, 1913

Resident at: Specialty Care Mississauga Road, Mississauga, Ontario (at her death in 2007)

Keys to enjoying her later years: Having support from her family, friends, and caregivers; composing music; writing, believing in religion; having a sense of humour; learning new skills; living with passion

Why in a long-term care home: Assistance required because of arthritic knees and failing vision; ability to follow her passions; making new friends of residents and staff

≈

I received an email from Justine Welburn, Director of Resident Services at Specialty Care Mississauga Road on February 14, 2007. The email read: "Hello Irene, I have just received information from the OLTCA on your upcoming initiative. I was very excited about the premise of your project and have a few residents in mind for you to meet. Unfortunately we just lost a resident who would have been perfect for you. I am wondering if you are still able to include her somehow?"

After thinking about it for a while I decided to have the late Eleanor Mary Russell (née Ellis) be a part of the photo exhibit and the book, as her legacy is very important. Her kindness, creativity, passion for living, and bonds with family and friends live on after her demise. The gifts she leaves behind are precious.

Eleanor studied at the Royal Conservatory of Music in Toronto and wrote her first piece of music at the age of sixteen. She also wrote stories and poetry throughout her life. At eighty-eight years of age, after writing music for more than seventy years, she had a CD produced. It was called *Moments of Praise, Moments of Memories.*

I decided to include in this piece the poem that Eleanor wrote for her funeral service, as well as the eulogy given by her daughter, Wendy Johnson, and a piece written by her granddaughter Heather Johnson. Who better to talk about Eleanor's life than Wendy, Heather, and Eleanor herself?

Eulogy by Eleanor's Daughter, Wendy Johnson
Eleanor Mary (Ellis) Russell
July 5, 1913–January 25, 2007

Thank you to all of you for your presence with us today. John and I are comforted to be surrounded by so many of our family and friends as we take on the role of the older generation. Thank you, Catherine, for your compassion and care in preparing this service and for including Mom's poem that she wrote for herself. She revised it only last month. Ken Anderson, a Thedford boy, who also took part in the service, grew up with John and spent countless hours at the farm enjoying Mom's cakes, pies, and chili. We are grateful to my pastor, John Tapscott, for his ministry to our family in the last days of Mom's life.

Mom did not want a eulogy at her funeral. She loved the words of the Anglican Prayer Book and wanted only the funeral service from it. She wanted the focus of the service to be on the Lord and not on her. However, we felt that we wanted to say something about her life too, and this has not interfered with the solemnity of the service, so "Sorry Mom!"

Eleanor Mary Ellis was born in London, Ontario, on July 5, 1913, to Ethel and Arthur Ellis. Her childhood years were spent in Petrolia, where her father was the editor of the newspaper, the *Advertiser-Topic*. She had an older sister, Marion. Because of family problems Mom moved in her teens with her mother to London to live with her grandmother. She studied piano and voice at the Royal Conservatory in Toronto, where she went each week for lessons. She moved to Toronto for a year and made her debut into Toronto society.

At that time she spent most of her spare time playing bridge, riding horses, and going to dances as well as practising music. She always looked back at this period of her life as being a waste of time! The family had a cottage at Ipperwash beach and spent the summers there. Mom went to dances at the casino, where a young man named Mac Russell was playing the violin and piano. Their mutual love of music brought them together, and they married on October 6, 1937. Mom, the city girl with no experience in cooking or rural life, went to live on the Russell family farm, not only with her husband but with his two elderly uncles as well. She was surrounded by encouraging neighbours and new relatives who made the transition easier for her. Twin daughters died at birth in 1942. I was born the following year and John in 1945.

As a new bride, Mom quickly learned to do all of the things farmers' wives and mothers of small children do, and the fifty-five years she lived on the farm were

her happiest. She drove the tractor, pitted cherries, pickled, canned, cooked for threshings, planted a garden, cut the heads off chickens. She made clothes for us, knitted socks for the war effort, drove us to music lessons, supported the school concerts, and took us to church where she played the organ. Nothing out of the ordinary in those things, but she did more. She wrote a book called *That You Might Believe*, and also wrote music — mainly Christian songs, but others as well. One I remember was a long epic about a sultan who had a flea under his turban! After seventy years of writing music, her CD, *Moments of Praise, Moments of Memories*, was produced in 2001, a wonderful legacy to our family and a blessing to many others.

Mom made many friends of all ages over the years. Her sense of humour and love of people have brought joy to many. I have been privileged to have had my grandmother, my aunt, and my mother as excellent role models in how to grow old without resentment, how to look for the good in people, and how to make lives brighter for others. The emails I've received since her death are full of happy memories that we will cherish. My friend Shirley reminded me that in the days before credit cards, Mom always carried a $2 bill in her bra, just in case.

Mom's move to Specialty Care in Mississauga in April 2005 was her choice, and she embraced this last part of her life with the same enthusiasm as she did all things. Latterly she was hampered by arthritic knees and failing vision, but with the help of the caring staff and good friends she continued to make a contribution to life. We were grateful that so many new people came into her life that loved her and cared for her. She wrote a birthday song for the home and set Wilfred Campbell's poem "Indian Summer" to music. When we bought her a laptop computer she was excited about learning something new and, although frustrated with it at times, decided it was a useful tool for helping with the articles she continued to write.

In the morning of the day she went to the hospital, I sat quietly with her while she proofread her latest writing. We were blessed that she was doing what the wanted right up to the end.

We were very fortunate to have a mother and grandmother who prayed for her children and grandchildren. Nothing can be more important. Her three granddaughters, Heather, Katherine, and Martha, enriched her life immeasurably.

January 29, 2007, Gilpin Funeral Chapel,
Thedford, Ontario, Canada

Reflection by Eleanor's Granddaughter Heather Johnson

My grandmother, Eleanor Russell, was a wonderful role model for how to grow old gracefully. She didn't complain about getting older, and that was likely because she said she never felt her age. Even into her nineties she said she still felt nineteen! For years, doctors, family, and friends had told her to slow down, but it was not in her to sit and do nothing. In her later years when her knees gave her trouble she was never sitting idly around. Her room at the long-term care centre was filled with her various tasks … books that she was reading, knitting needles and yarn for making dishcloths, and stacks of papers and her laptop computer for writing her latest project.…

My grandmother always enjoyed composing and playing music, writing articles, and reading. Though she got great pleasure from these pastimes, she always found time to help others. In her younger years on the farm she drove friends who were unable to drive themselves, played the church organ, taught Sunday School, and cooked and baked for family and friends. Her focus was always on others and not on herself. She left her life's path to God.

Those who knew her, even if only for a short time, saw her generous spirit. I am blessed to have had a grandmother who passed on her faith in God and her enthusiasm for life, not only to her family but also to everyone around her.

April 7, 2007

Be Glad For Me

Be glad for me, the brightest sun
Is lighting my eternal Day.
The dearest Voice I've ever heard
Has called me on my homeward way.
Be glad for me, I know His Word.
Believing whosoever came to God
Through Christ, would surely find
New Life Eternal through his Name.
Be glad for me: and be rejoiced
That ere my spirit heard Him call.
In rapturous faith I came to Christ
Whose strength would never let me fall.
Be glad for me: the happiest days
I'll ever know are just ahead.
You see the sunset of my life

I'll see the promise of glory instead.
Be glad for me, but hear me now:
To follow Christ through life is sweet
Commit your way to God and trust
And let him make your life complete.
Then, when in *your* turn, you hear
His calling Voice from heaven above,
You also, with your eyes on Christ
Will rise in Resurrection love.

Eleanor Russell
Copyright 1990, revisited in 2006 one month prior to
her death

Profile 17

∽

PHILIP O. McHALE

Philip O. McHale doing woodwork outside at the Garden Terrace, Nepean, Ontario.

Philip O. McHale

Offset printing employee, clarinet, drum, saxophone and piano hobbyist, wood carver, tuck-shop operator, father, grandfather.

Born: Ottawa, Ontario, 1936
Home: Garden Terrace, Nepean, Ontario

ASSISTANCE WITH RESPONSIBILITIES

"We would not have been able to remain in our own home safely due to my mini-strokes and a triple bypass and my wife Theresa's deterioration due to multiple sclerosis. If we would have remained in our own home, my health would have deteriorated faster as I was the prime caregiver. By moving into the nursing home, I now can enjoy the latter part of my life and the life that my wife and I share together. So many of our responsibilities have been removed and we still have some health left."

I believe it is important to:

- "Realize that life in a nursing home can be better than life in the community but the problem is often the negative image that nursing homes have"
- "Understand that when a loved one is in a nursing home it relieves a lot of the pressure placed on children or the spouse-caregiver, as they will feel more comfortable knowing parent or spouse is being properly cared for"
- "Pursue your passion"

April 2007

History: Offset printing employee, musical hobbyist, woodcarver, tuck shop operator, father, grandfather

Born: Ottawa, Ontario, 1936

Currently resident at: Garden Terrace (Omni Health Care), Nepean, Ontario

Keys to enjoying his later years: Using the extra time available to pursue his passions; enjoying family and his remaining years with his wife; accepting his current limitations; remaining active

Why in a long-term care home: Having the needed support such as meals, medical care, and activities for both himself and wife; not having to be (or have their children be) the prime caregiver for his wife

Philip was born in Ottawa, Ontario, in 1936 to Rose and James McHale. There were four boys in the family and three girls; in order of birth they were Therese, Michael, Francis, Helen, Danny, Patrick, and Philip.

Philip went to St. Bridgett (Bridger) Elementary School and then completed Grade 9 at the Ottawa Technical School. He left school after Grade 9 at age fifteen to help support his family, as his father had become blind (he was a printer and had cataracts). Philip came from a very poor family, and after his father's situation changed his mother, Rose, had to support her children by cleaning houses.

At age fifteen, Philip began work as a delivery boy for a drugstore and then worked for a furniture company. His next job was working in the Ottawa Civic Hospital, where he was employed for the next forty-eight years, from 1953 to 2001. He worked as an offset printer, a skill he had learned at the Ottawa Technical School.

Philip met his wife, Theresa, when he was thirteen years old and she was eleven. He married her seven years later. Prior to their marriage, Theresa worked for one year at Helene Curtis doing office work. She had developed multiple sclerosis at seventeen. Despite her condition, Theresa and Philip had three children: Philip Jr., James, and Cathy, who between them have produced four grandchildren.

Philip was involved in raising the children, and he also had several hobbies, including playing the clarinet, the saxophone, the piano, and the drums. This passion for music has remained with him throughout his life.

Initially Theresa was able to walk with the help of a cane, but as her condition became worse she began to use a wheelchair. When the children were young, Philip and Theresa had home care provided by Community Care Access Centre, which continued to provide assistance and services once the children grew up and left their parents' home.

Life wasn't always easy for the family, but when the children became older the family was able to travel to Barbados, where a friend of Philip's let them stay at his place. These were cherished times for the family, and Philip treasures the memories.

Regarding being in a long-term care home Philip said, "I should have done it ten years ago." Philip now uses a walker. After the children grew up and left, Philip and Theresa had a house, but there were too many responsibilities. Theresa had medical care, but it was too hard for Philip to lift her and maintain the household. Philip was becoming disoriented and had a few mini-strokes, and then he had a triple bypass operation.

Philip was worried about Theresa. Who would take care of her? Philip moved into the long-term care home first to see what it would be like. Theresa was terrified of moving to a long-term care home, largely because of the negative image of life there. Philip said that it took only a short while before they both saw that life in a long-term care home was the answer to their situation. They have found that the meals are good, their laundry is done for them, and they have medical and nursing care. Their children live in the Ottawa area, and they are able to visit their parents and take them out quite frequently. The family is still very much a part of one another's lives.

When asked about the positive aspects of aging, Philip said he can still play his musical instruments and has more time to pursue his passions. He does woodworking and is becoming more competent at it.

Their long-term care home has a minibus given to them by the Ontario government that is shared by two other homes, so the residents are able to go on may outings, including baseball and hockey games, Christmas and other holiday dinners, the Canadian War Museum, movies, and the Royal Canadian Mint.

Philip runs the tuck shop, for which he takes a cart around to residents with crossword puzzles and books.

He is the president of the Residents' Council, which meets monthly, plans outings, and looks at problems in the long-term care home; it is run by management with the assistance of the residents.

When asked about leaving thoughts for future generations, Philip said he feels a project like this is so important: there is life in long-term care homes, and when a loved one is in a long-term care home it relieves a lot of the pressure placed on the caregivers. He said that a book is needed to show what life in a long-term care home is really like. He can stay with his wife, it is affordable, and their children live close enough to visit.

"I feel that this book will give the public a better understanding of what life in a nursing home is really like and that they do not need to be afraid," he said. "Living in a nursing home can be a positive experience. I feel that moving into the Garden Terrace in Kanata, Ontario, really helped to relieve all the pressures and responsibilities of owning a home and being a caregiver to my wife, who has multiple sclerosis. The public tends to have a negative view towards nursing homes, and hopefully this book will show otherwise. This book could shed a positive light on nursing homes from someone who is living in one with his wife. My views on nursing homes certainly changed when I moved in. I have a great quality of life. I think that it would be a good idea to have this type of book available to people who are making the decision to place a loved one in a nursing home as the views are coming from the people who are experiencing it first-hand."

Profile 18

COLLEEN TAFFE

Colleen Taffe reflects.
Cardinal Ambrozic Houses of Providence,
Providence Healthcare, Scarborough, Ontario.

Colleen Taffe

High school graduate, painter, hobbyist, explorer, movie enthusiast, mother.

Born: Toronto, Ontario, Canada, 1967
Home: Cardinal Ambrozic Houses of Providence, Providence Healthcare, Scarborough, Ontario

LEARN FROM MY MISTAKES

"Don't do drugs! I was naïve, young and alone.

"I am paying the consequences and I feel that I would have gone in the same direction even if I had more contact with my parents when I was growing up. I do not blame them for my situation. I still have a rebellious streak and this gives me strength. I am happy now and have found inner peace. My soul is peaceful and that is all that counts. I go out into the community with my scooter. I go to movies and meet friends and see my children occasionally. I would be afraid to live in the community — I feel safer living at Providence Centre."

I believe it is important to:

- "Accept my situation and forgive myself"
- "Be able to cope despite adversities in life"
- "Believe in God"
- "Do different things despite limitations"
- "Feel safe and familiar"
- "Enjoy facilities, including religious opportunities"

March 2007

History: high school graduate, painter, hobbyist, explorer, movie enthusiast, mother

Born: Toronto, Ontario, 1967

Currently resident at: Cardinal Ambrozic Houses of Providence, Scarborough, Ontario

Keys to enjoying her life: Having support from her family; making new friends; continuing to learn; painting; participating in various activities; coping and being proud of her survival; believing in God

Why in a long-term care home: Physical and emotional support from the staff due to her mobility and speech impairments; the comfort of feeling safe and in a familiar environment

⌁

Colleen was one of five sisters, of which she was the youngest. Her older sisters were Cecile, Sandra, Pat, and Jackie. When Colleen was born, her parents were extremely busy working and trying to provide the necessities that the children needed. Colleen said that her parents were not around very much and she was raised largely by her neighbours: "raised by the street," as she described it. She had a good relationship with the neighbours, and her memories of that time in her life are very positive.

She described herself as being a "brainer," as she was very smart and did well in school. She attended Warden Street Public School until Grade 8, and she was involved in track and field events both at school and off campus.

Colleen did well in high school and graduated Grade 12. She was involved in the school's production of *Othello*, and had several friends.

Colleen's parents were always busy, but she remained close with her sisters. The entire family would eat their meal together on Sunday morning; this was a special family time.

Colleen explained that after she graduated high school, her childhood got away from her. She worked at McDonald's and did some telemarketing. Unfortunately, she was negatively influenced by some of her friends, and she tried using marijuana. Later, she began to use heroin. Her parents were very disappointed in her.

She lost her job in her twenties, and life went downhill from there. She was in a shelter for women in North York called the 21 Shelter. Colleen had no one to turn to and had to make difficult decisions, including becoming a prostitute, which she now regrets, about how to finance her drug addiction. Eventually, Colleen overdosed on heroin and could not be found for twenty-four hours.

She ended up at the Toronto General Hospital in very bad shape. The overdosing left her with mobility and speech impairments. She was moved to Providence Healthcare's long-term care home, the Cardinal Ambrozic Houses of Providence, and has lived there for the last ten years. Her sisters visit occasionally, as do her parents. She also has a son, Andre, and a daughter, Shannon, who visit occasionally. They were raised by her parents. Andre is studying to be a nurse and hopes to attend medical school and become a doctor.

Colleen has grown used to living at Providence. She doesn't know anything else. She feels safe there, and it is familiar to her. She has gotten to know many people who come and spend the end of their lives here. Although she knows new residents will take their places when they pass on, Colleen misses the friends she has made over the years.

Colleen has an electric wheelchair, and she enjoys going out; it is an adventure for her. She uses Wheel Trans to go to movies and for shopping at Scarborough Town Centre. She also goes to Variety Village and swims there. She does art classes at Providence and loves to paint.

She has become more religious at Providence and goes to High Gospel Services every Sunday. She finds that this offers her strength and forgiveness. She has grown to accept her situation and has forgiven herself.

Colleen said she felt dirty on the outside and on the inside before. She felt dirty on the outside because she did not take care of herself properly, and on the inside because her spirit was unclean. She described herself as being shy and said she would walk with her head held down. Now she holds her head high because she is proud that she has survived and changed her attitude towards life. She feels that religion and having faith in a loving and forgiving God has helped her to heal. She feels clean now — "as white as snow" — because of God.

When asked about what matters to her she said her strength and her ability to cope despite adversities in life. She is happy now and has found inner peace.

Profile 19

RUTH
ADAMS

*Ruth Adams working in her amazing garden
at Extendicare Oshawa, Ontario.*

Ruth Adams

Left high school to help with her younger siblings, housewife, rug-maker, embroiderer, award-winning gardener, wife, mother, grandmother, great-grandmother.

Born: Delta, Ontario, Canada, 1917
Home: Extendicare, Oshawa

THE GIFT OF GARDENING

"When I was a young girl, someone gave me a package of morning glory seeds. This was depression time so a small gift meant so much. I planted the seeds in some earth and when they bloomed their colour brought some life to the railway station where my family was living. This was the beginning of a lifetime passion for gardening, which still sustains me while living in a long-term care home. Every winter I am busy thinking about and planning next summer's garden. I give seeds and plants from my garden to others. I share the beauty and the joy!"

I believe it is important to:

- "Maintain a positive and passionate attitude to life"
- "Be concerned about others"
- "Be open to receiving family support"
- "Believe in God"
- "Stay involved, socialize and continue to be creative"
- "Not interfere with your child's choice of marital partner"

August 2007

History: Housewife, rug maker, embroiderer, award-winning gardener, wife, mother, grandmother, great-grandmother

Born: Delta, Ontario, 1917

Currently resident in: Extendicare Oshawa, Oshawa, Ontario

Keys to enjoying her later years: A positive attitude toward life; belief in religion; gardening; socializing with family and friends

Why in a long-term care home: The need for assistance because of various infirmities; the freedom to pursue her interests (especially gardening); physical and emotional support

～

Ruth's mother, Jessie Ellen Sopher, married her father, Herman Mallory Snider, and they had seven children: Ruth, Opal, Phyllis, Agatha, Jerald, Alwyn, and Victor.

Ruth had two sisters who were athletic, but this did not interest her. She liked to embroider. She had a hope chest, and she made several lovely items that she kept in the chest until she was married.

Ruth's father worked on the railway, and therefore the family never lived in one place for any length of time. They lived at the railway stations in the Ontario communities of North Bay, Brockville, Ottawa, and Delta. Her mother was kept busy raising the children.

When Ruth was a young girl someone gave her a package of morning glory seeds. She planted them near the railway station where the family was living, and they grew into lovely plants. This was the beginning of Ruth's passion for gardening, which has helped sustain her throughout her life, especially while living at Extendicare Oshawa. A small gift given to a child may remain a passion for the rest of her or his life.

Ruth first went to school at four years of age, as she attended with her older sister Opal. She left school at age fourteen as she had to help her mother with the other children. She got married at seventeen to Stanley Maurice Adams. At eighteen she had a son, Jack Mallory. Times were hard during the Depression, and they lived on beans and dandelion salad and rice. Stanley's mother ran a general store where Stanley worked. Ruth and Stanley had a second son, James Stanley, immediately after the Second World War. They also had a daughter, Sheila Mae, who was born in 1948.

The family lived in Amable, near Bancroft, at this time. Ruth did not work outside the home as she was busy raising the children. Stanley worked variety of jobs to make ends meet: he drove a school bus, worked in the woods cutting down trees, and prepared meals for the people who worked in the railroads.

When the children grew older and moved out of the family home in Whitby, where they had lived for thirty-five years, Stanley would hike, fish, and play baseball. Ruth made rugs, embroidered, and gardened. Ruth has won awards for gardening, and her work has been pictured in newspapers.

She has thirteen grandchildren and fifteen great-grandchildren.

Ruth and Stanley came to Extendicare Oshawa together. Ruth had colon cancer and a hip replacement prior to going into the long-term care home. Caring for Stanley at home was difficult for her. She said that after making meals for seventeen years for her very particular husband, coming to a long-term care home was a positive experience. Her meals are prepared and her medications are monitored.

Ruth feels that religion has helped her with the difficulties that life has presented, and has also helped her with the loss of Stanley, who died of pneumonia in 2007.

When she came to Extendicare Oshawa, Ruth looked out her window one day and saw a pile of pebbles, rocks, and pine needles and decided to continue with her childhood passion. Gradually over the years she turned the area into an extraordinary perennial garden; she began it in her mid eighties and continues to nurture it in her nineties. The garden is so beautiful that people come from neighbouring towns and from Toronto to see it! She feels that people become depressed when they are not busy, and the garden is a remedy and provides happiness for her.

When asked what wisdom she wants to share with others she said one should marry whom one wants. She did not interfere with her children's choice of marital partners. She and Stanley tried to raise them well and that way hopefully they are able to make wise decisions in life now. She also feels that television is bad for children. Things were more modest when she was young.

She also shared some thoughts about her life at Extendicare Oshawa. She was very much afraid of having Stanley die at home while she was caring for him, and she feels that the fact that they were living in a long-term care home when he died was ideal. She had the support she so needed, as they were both elderly at the time of his death.

Ruth continues to live life to its fullest. She maintains the garden each season and continues to have people visit her. Some are her children and grandchildren, some are friends from the past, and many are new people who come to see her amazing garden. She is still passionate about living!

Profile 20

BRUCE E. HUTCHESON

Bruce Hutcheson is a war veteran. This photo was taken in his room at Christie Gardens, Toronto.

Bruce E. Hutcheson

Second World War veteran, mechanic for Metro Toronto police department, swimming volunteer, husband, father, grandfather, great-grandfather.

Born: Toronto, Ontario, Canada, 1917
Home: Christie Gardens, Toronto

THE NEED TO BE AT PEACE

"Living at Christie Gardens takes away from the 'what ifs' in life. What if I fall and no one knows? I am safer here.

"The wisdom I offer to younger people is that it is important to work together for world peace. There is also a need to be at peace with yourself as you face death. But for now I continue to live. I even have a sister living at Christie Gardens and a few other relatives. I feel fortunate. I'm not alone."

I believe it is important to:

- "Be at peace with yourself as you face death"
- "Volunteer your time to activities of others"
- "Develop close relationships of trust and friendship with those friends and family you care for"

March 2007

History: Second World War army veteran, mechanic for Toronto Police Service, volunteer, husband, father, grandfather, great-grandfather

Born: Toronto, Ontario, 1917

Currently resident at: Christie Gardens, Toronto, Ontario

Keys to enjoying his later years: Being at peace with himself; taking part in a variety of activities; remaining in contact with friends and family

Why in a long-term care home: Having support to deal with the physical infirmities caused by knee replacements and hearing loss; socializing with other residents, staff, and relatives who also live in the home

When I met Bruce he had just turned ninety the day before. He was born on Clinton Street in Toronto to Ethel and John Hutcheson.

Bruce attended the Essex Street Public School before going to Harbord Collegiate. While attending school he had newspaper routes for both the *Toronto Telegram* and the *Toronto Star*. Bruce had to leave high school before graduation because his father became ill and he had to go out to work. His first job was in a gas station, and then in 1941 he started working on an assembly line for the Ford Motor Company on Danforth Avenue, where he assembled mostly trucks for the army.

Bruce knew he was going to be drafted, so he joined the army in 1942; he married Maisie in the same year and then immediately left for England. When Sicily was successfully invaded he was sent to a reinforcement camp in Italy until 1944. (He laughed when he recalled that while in Italy, he got a letter from his mother telling him he had been drafted.) He was then shipped to Holland, and after the war was won he moved to Germany with the occupation army. In 1946 he came home to Canada.

When asked about his impressions of the war he said it was a good life but also a dangerous one, as he was in combat zones all the time. He was in the Army Public Relations unit for four years. The unit did film and photography for the newspapers and other media and also included war correspondents and the propaganda unit. Bruce's role in the unit was to maintain the Jeeps, and he had three mechanics that reported to him. He also dispatched the drivers and vehicles. The war correspondents and photographers had their favourite drivers and they would often go out as a team. Sometimes when the unit got stuck for a photographer, they would send Bruce out with a camera, since he was also a mechanic and would be an asset to the team. Once a broadcast van was sent up close to the line, and to scare the enemy it broadcast that the division would attack, but in reality the division was over in Holland and in no position to attack at that location!

Another function of the Army Public Relations unit was publishing the *Maple Leaf Newspaper*, which was done by a separate group within the unit. This paper was printed in Rome, Naples, and Amsterdam, and it reported on what was happening in the war as well as news from back home in Canada. One of the correspondents Bruce worked with was Ruth Carmichael, who worked for the *Toronto Telegram* and whose father was the mayor of Collingwood.

Since this was a non-combative unit, they did not lose too many men and women. The few people they lost were drivers who went closer to the front on assignment. Other infantry units that were closer to the front lost more men who had to be replaced. The day before our interview, Bruce had a call from Dave King, a corporal in the film and photo section of Bruce's unit, who now lives in Kelowna, British Columbia. Another friend he has kept up with is Norm Quick, who was a photographer and now lives in Ottawa.

When Bruce returned home, he worked for a dry cleaner for a year and a half. Then he worked for the Toronto Police Service as a mechanic for thirty-three years until he retired. He is the past president of the Metro Toronto Police War Veterans Association. Bruce volunteered as a teacher at Oakwood Collegiate for the Mermaid's Swim Club. He was also involved with the Canadian Amateur Swimming Association as a certified timer, judge, and starter. He officiated at local and major swim meets, including the Canada Games and Pan-American Games.

Bruce and his wife, Maisie, had two children: Gordon, who lives in Ottawa, and Janet, who lives in Vancouver.

Gordon is married to Francoise and has two children, while Janet has no children.

Maisie worked as a payroll supervisor for the Foreign Affairs division at the Manufacturers Life Insurance Co. When Maisie worked, her mother helped care for the children.

As Bruce and Maisie grew older, they and their family decided that a long-term care home would be the wisest decision, as they were both ill and unable to cope with living on their own safely. Bruce had two knee replacements and uses a hearing aid due to suffering hearing loss from shelling when he was in the war. The home provides a variety of activities such as exercise classes, outside events, and visits to museums, galleries, and lectures.

Maisie passed away in August 2006 while she and Bruce were living at Christie Gardens. Bruce said he will feel at peace when his time is up. He feels that he has outlived his usefulness, although he wants to continue living. Bruce has other relatives, including a sister, who are living at Christie Gardens, which improves his life.

Christie Gardens is a multi-faith long-term care home, although it is primarily a Christian community, and it operates on a not-for-profit basis. Ed Clements provided pastoral care services and counselling before he left for a new position.

Profile 21

HELEN NILES

Helen Niles playing cards at Extendicare, Lakefield, Ontario.

Helen Niles

Left Grade 11 to help family, domestic worker in family inn, caregiver to ailing husband, wife, mother, grandmother, great-grandmother.

Born: Halifax, Nova Scotia, Canada, 1915
Home: Extendicare-Lakefield Nursing Home, Lakefield

FEELING SAFE AND SECURE

"These are the things I like about the Extendicare-Lakefield: security, comfort, peace of mind, the church and outings, having my medication monitored, friendships I've made in the home, and Mya — the Golden Retriever! While living in a long-term care home, I receive the help I need, I feel safe and secure and I do not have to be a burden on my children. They see me on a regular basis but my health needs are being cared for by the staff at Extendicare-Lakefield Nursing Home."

I believe it is important to:

- "Recognize that life is what you make it"
- "Treat everyone the same as we all have much in common"
- "Try not to be a burden to your children"
- "Believe in God"
- "Always stay involved and socialize with others"
- "Enjoy activities"

April 2007

History: domestic worker in family inn, caregiver to ailing husband wife, mother, grandmother, great-grandmother

Born: Halifax, Nova Scotia, 1915

Home: Extendicare Lakefield, Lakefield, Ontario

Keys to enjoying her later years: Support from her family and friends; attending church services; playing euchre with friends; not being a burden to her family; recognizing that life is what you make of it

Why in a long-term care home: Support required due to her failing eyesight and hearing and her limited mobility; great peace of mind; readily available activities; comfort provided by the facility's dog, Mya

Helen's mother's name was Jean and her father's name was Gordon. Helen was the eldest of four children. Her siblings were Catherine, Jean, and Gordon Jr.

When asked if her childhood was happy, Helen responded by saying that the family moved around a lot as her father was in the navy. They lived in Montreal, Quebec; Halifax, Nova Scotia; Depot Harbour, Ontario; and Cobourg, Ontario. On one hand, all of the moving around was difficult, but on the other hand, she feels that it helped her and her siblings as they were forced to become more confident and outgoing.

Once the family settled in Cobourg, Helen attended high school at Cobourg Collegiate. Eventually her father left the navy and the family bought a bed and breakfast, the St. Lawrence Hotel, which they renamed Kelly's Home Like Inn. Historically, the inn was actually a stagecoach stop where the horses were watered. Helen finished Grade 11 and then began to help with the family business. Today Helen's nephew Gordon is still running the business.

Stephen Niles was a guest who boarded at the inn, where Helen met him. In 1937, when Helen was twenty-two, they were married. Stephen was born and grew up in Cobourg. He worked as a foreman at Cooey Machine and Arms in Cobourg for forty-seven years. The United States bought the factory, and it became Winchester Arms. Helen and Stephen had two children: Rosemary, who was a nurse and is retired now, and Greg, who works at the Bank of Montreal. Helen has five granddaughters and nine great-grandchildren.

Helen said that her positive attitude towards life comes from moving around so much. Although she was shy when she was a young girl, she was meeting people all the time and she learned to be friendly; she became even more extroverted while working in the inn. Interacting with many people on a regular basis helped her to develop self-confidence.

Helen did not work after she got married until her son Greg was twelve years old. She then worked at a Sears order office, at General Foods in advertising, and later at McIntosh's Fabric and Drapery Store.

In 1988, Helen and Stephen left Cobourg and moved to Peterborough to an apartment. In 1997, Stephen began to show signs of having Alzheimer's disease. They were able to stay together and in their own apartment with services provided by Community Care Access Centre; they received one hour per day, five days a week.

Helen received help with such things as bathing, taking medication, shopping, and house cleaning. The caregivers would even take Stephen out for a walk while Helen took care of her own needs. Stephen remained at home with Helen until a few days before he died in 2001. Helen said that he was a wonderful husband. He retired at sixty-five and lived until he was ninety.

Following Stephen's death, Helen moved to the Peterborough Manor Retirement Residence, where she lived from 2001 to 2006. She chose this area to live in as it was close to her daughter. Her son, Greg, lives in Toronto; he phones her every night and visits every month. When Helen's health began to deteriorate she decided it was time to receive more care and she made the move to Extendicare Lakefield Nursing Home. Helen has a kidney stone that cannot be operated on. Her eyesight is failing, she has two hearing aids, and she uses a walker to ambulate.

Helen said that living in a long-term care home cuts down on the "what ifs." She finds that she has greater peace of mind.

Before she moved into the long-term care home, she believed it would be like a hospital and she had visions of being in bed all the time. She kicked up a fuss when her daughter told her that she felt Helen would be better living in a long-term care home. Eight weeks later she adjusted, and now she is enjoying her life. She said that it's not like being in your own home, but the facility she lives in is the best that it can be for her, given her age and health issues. She said that she is very satisfied.

Before I arrived to interview Helen, she had already prepared a list of things that she was enjoying in the home. The list included security; comfort; peace of mind; not being a burden on her family; church services; outings; musical events; medication; friendships; Mya, the golden retriever; exercise; hymn sing chapel; bingo; art therapy; baking; crafts; planting; gardening; and friendships.

Helen has found that she has a lot in common with other residents. Before she felt she should stay away because they were sick, but she realized she was wrong. Helen enjoys playing euchre with a number of residents at the long-term care home.

When asked what words of wisdom she could provide for future generations she said that life is what you make of it. Things happen in life for a reason and it is what one does with the challenges. Also, things could always be worse.

Profile 22

LUONG
VIEN

Luong Vien shown doing early-morning exercises at the O'Neill Centre, Toronto.

Luong Vien

Worker in traditional Chinese pharmacy, Vietnamese boat refugee, garment industry worker, exercise enthusiast.

Born: Anping, Vietnam, 1928
Home: O'Neill Centre, Toronto

NOT FEAR IMPENDING DEATH

"Religion has helped me. In Canada I became a Buddhist and this religion has helped me find inner peace. My religious feelings became stronger when I came to Canada from Vietnam because in Vietnam I did not encounter religion as much but when I moved to Canada and lived with my brother I began to read the bible. I trust the Buddhist teachings and they have helped me not fear my impending death. I feel I will be at peace once my time is up but for now I am living life to its fullest with a feeling of gratitude."

I believe it is important to:

- "Try to maintain a happy attitude to life"
- "Accept support from family, friends and staff"
- "Be religious"
- "Keep a routine and exercise as much as you can to the best of your ability"

May 2007

History: Worker in traditional Chinese pharmacy, Vietnamese boat refugee, garment industry worker, exerciser

Born: Anping, Vietnam, 1928

Home: O'Neill Centre, Toronto, Ontario

Keys to enjoying her later years: Support from her family; belief in the Buddhist religion; maintaining a happy attitude towards life

Why in a long-term care home: Physical and emotional support from the staff; the comfort of feeling safe; the meals provided to her; various programs offered (especially the movies)

⚊

Luong was born in Vietnam. Her father's name was Zuo Vien, and her mother's name was Zhi Tong. Both of Luong's parents were born in China and then moved to Vietnam. Luong had three sisters and five brothers. Two of her brothers passed away when they were young.

Luong speaks Mandarin and Cantonese. I was fortunate enough to have Ping Wang, Food Services Manager at the O'Neill Centre, interpret for me during our interview.

Luong's mother never worked, as she was involved in raising her children. Luong had a very happy childhood, which may be the reason that she is content and happy in her later life. Her father made metal tools that were used in gardening, kitchen supplies, etc. The family

lived in a city, and her father's work provided them with enough food to eat. Luong attended school for five years, from ages nine to fourteen. There was one teacher in a one-room schoolhouse. When the Second World War began Luong had to stop going to school.

During the war, the family's life continued on as before, but after the war nobody was buying tools so the children had to go out and work. Luong was able to find a job working in a traditional Chinese pharmacy packaging herbs.

Luong came to Canada in 1979 after leaving her job in the pharmacy. She had liked this job but eventually had to leave work to stay home and help her elderly mother cook, clean, do laundry, and take care of her younger brothers. Her two older brothers had left for China and never returned during the time of the Chinese Cultural Revolution, led by China's ruling Communist Party. She never saw her brothers again and believes that they were never able to leave China.

In 1979 the Communist Party came to Vietnam. Her mother and father were too old to come to Canada, so Luong and her brother and his family came over on a boat. They were referred to as the boat refugees.

Luong and her family sailed to the Philippines from Vietnam, and then Canada paid for the refugees to fly to Canada. For the first twenty days, the government put the refugees up in a hotel. Then Luong, her brother, and his family lived in a church in Toronto for three years. Eventually her brother bought a home for his family and Luong was able to live with them. She worked on Spadina and Queen in the garment industry for four years and then she was laid off. She found her second job in the garment industry and sewed labels for six years until she retired in 1989 at the age of sixty.

Luong spoke about the fact that she never married. She did have a proposal but she said he was much younger than she was, as she looks much younger and he did not know her true age. When Luong was of marrying age, the war was on and she did not think about marriage due to the circumstances. Just surviving was a priority. As the years passed by and she moved to Canada, she never found anyone to marry.

While Luong lived with her brother and his family, she paid them rent and she cooked for herself. She had security living with her brother but also independence.

After a fall in the bathroom that nobody was aware of, as well as her advancing years, she felt that it was time to move to a long-term care home. It was her decision. She said that she has had a happy attitude all of her life, even when making that decision. Religion has helped. In Canada she became a Buddhist, which has helped her find inner peace. Luong lives with these teachings, and she has a calm and peaceful approach towards life.

Luong sees her brother on a regular basis as she is invited to his home to visit the family. Her brother has power of attorney for her affairs, and they have a very good relationship.

Luong loves living at the O'Neill Centre and sees it as her home. She shares a room with three other women, and she is comfortable with this arrangement. She is not able to afford a single room. Every day she gets up at 5:30 a.m., dresses, watches the news on the television, and receives her medication from the nurse. Then she exercises to keep her body and mind healthy. This helps her to feel more relaxed.

Luong likes the food at the centre. She enjoys the programs, especially the movies. She goes to sleep at 9:30 each night but never sleeps during the day.

Profile 23

ALAN PHILP

Alan Philp playing the drums at Community Nursing Home, Pickering, Ontario.

Alan Philp

Grammar school graduate, executive at Pilkington Glass Co., drummer, husband, father, grandfather, great-grandfather.

Born: Dundee, Scotland, U.K., 1929
Home: Community Nursing Home, Pickering

CONTINUE TO FOLLOW YOUR DREAM

"When I lived in England, I had some drums that I loved playing. When I moved to Canada I could not afford to bring them and I never bought another set. Now while living in a long-term care home and thanks to a volunteer, my dream of playing the drums has come true.

"The wisdom I offer to others is: it is important to keep on smiling. If you were lucky enough to be given more years to live, then use them wisely. No matter what the adversity, face it head on and say: no, you are not going to beat me!

"Forget our ethnic, tribal and religious differences. BE TOLERANT!"

I believe it is important to:

- "Socialize and make friends"
- "Be concerned about others"
- "Embrace family time and support"
- "Continue doing things and try to do new things"

May 2007

History: Grammar school graduate, executive at Pilkington Brothers Canada Ltd., drummer, husband, father, grandfather, great-grandfather

Born: Dundee, Scotland, 1929

Currently resident in: Community Nursing Home, Pickering, Ontario

Keys to enjoying his later years: Using the extra time available to enjoy his passions (such as playing drums), his hobbies (such as gardening and dog handling), and his family; maintaining a strong sense of triumphing over adversity

Why in a long-term care home: Having the needed support such as meals, medical care, and other essentials; outings and social activities giving relief from loneliness

Alan's mother, Elizabeth, and his father, John, also had another son, Arthur, and a daughter, Jean. Elizabeth was busy raising the three children while John was a civil servant who worked for His Majesty's Stationery Office. His father was wounded and lost a lung and had other wounds from the First World War.

Alan has happy memories of his early childhood. He lived in Dundee for the first three years of his life, but the family moved to London before the start of the Second World War, as Alan said that his father did not want to go down in the mines.

Alan went to the London School for Boys, which was a public school. He finished grammar school at age sixteen as the family could not afford to have him go to university. Alan played the drums as a hobby in his teenage years, and these were some of his happiest memories.

Alan has very vivid memories of "the Blitz" (1939 to 1945) when he was living in London. He said it was horrible. The family lived in a two-storey house, but they slept under the beds. The bombs and later the rockets that rained down all around them in London during these years spared their home but caused immense damage and loss of life around them. It was a very scary and difficult time. A good friend and neighbour of Alan was killed during the Blitz. There was food rationing, and the family had a ration book. His brother served in the army in Burma during this time.

When the war was over and everyone was celebrating VE Day in April 1945, he was in the crowd that was around Buckingham Palace.

After Alan left school he worked at the *Daily Sketch* in the photo news department for two years. Alan enlisted in the Air Force in 1947 and at the end of that year was shipped to Singapore. He left the air force in 1949.

Alan went to Canada House in England to apply to leave London. He arrived in Canada in 1951. He lived with his sister and brother-in-law (who had sponsored him) and began working for an English company, Pilkington Brothers Canada Ltd., which was his employer for the rest of his working life. He was transferred to Calgary and then to Saskatoon, where he was the office manager. In the 1960s, he was transferred back to Toronto. When Alan retired at age sixty-three in 1992, he was the treasurer at Pilkington Brothers.

Alan married in 1959. He met his wife, Joan, at a dance at Bessborough Hall in Saskatoon. She was also English. They had two sons who were born in Saskatoon: Keith and Robert, who has since passed away. He had three grandchildren and one great-grandchild at the time of the interview.

Alan was still living in his own home when he retired. After experiencing balance problems, he saw a neurologist and was diagnosed with a neurological illness. In order to get assistance, he moved in with his son, Keith, and his family when Joan passed away in 1999.

Alan came to the Community Nursing Home facility in 2005. He could not remain with Keith's family as he needed assistance in toileting and other essentials. He and his son chose Community Nursing Home partly because it is close to Keith. Alan also liked the programs, socializing, and trips offered there. He finds the socializing and the ability to make friends provides relief from the loneliness he suffered from prior to coming into the home. His hobbies, which he can still indulge at the home, include stained glass, anything to do with dogs (both show and pets), and gardening, as well as the opportunity to exercise the long-held aspiration of playing drums.

When Alan left England he could not take his drums, as they were too expensive to ship. Throughout his life he wanted to play, but life intruded upon that dream. Now in a long-term care home he is following the lead of his idol, Gene Krupa, who was a big band drummer in the 1920s to 1960s. When Alan expressed a desire to play the drums a nurse named Sherry arranged for her son's set of drums, no longer used, to be brought into the facility. He plays with one of the entertainers who arrive at the home every Wednesday night to play for the residents. Alan's dreams have been fulfilled.

When asked about the positive aspects of aging, Alan said it was important to keep on smiling. If you are given more years to live, then use them wisely.

Alan is described as being "seventy-eight years young" by the staff at Community Nursing Home.

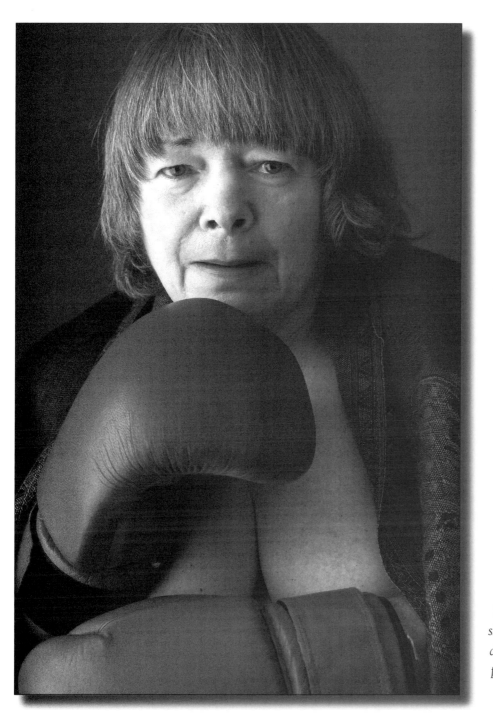

Profile 24

~

SHARON
DYER

*Sharon Dyer is shown with boxing gloves —
she has had quite a fight due to her Parkinson's
disease but she is still a woman, still alive, and
proud of it!! Photo taken at Craiglee Nursing
Home, Scarborough, Ontario.*

Sharon Dyer

Actress, singer, playwright, secretary, skier, biker, photographer, handicrafter, avid reader, and volunteer.

Born: Toronto, Ontario, Canada, 1941
Home: Craiglee Nursing Home, Scarborough, Ontario

JUST LIKE PEOPLE ANYWHERE

"I've been a fighter my whole life. I've had to be. Then, in 1984, I was diagnosed with young-onset Parkinson's disease. Without fighting, I would not be alive today. When life presents new challenges, my sense of humour saves me. The people here in the nursing home are just like people anywhere: they laugh and cry, fall in love and have sex just like people on the outside. We go out with friends, use Wheel Trans and complain about how it's always too late or too early. And I get around to many places on my four-wheeled scooter.

"My boyfriend — yes anything is possible at my age — is 66. He says the reason he sticks around is my sense of fun and the way I laugh. He calls me his hottie."

I believe it is important to:

- "Have a strong belief in yourself"
- "Have a sense of humour"
- "Maintain friendships"

October 2007

History: actress, singer, playwright, secretary, skier, biker, photographer, handicrafter, avid reader, volunteer

Born: Toronto, Ontario, 1941

Currently resident at: Craiglee Nursing Home, Scarborough, Ontario

Keys to enjoying her later years: Being a fighter and a survivor; believing in herself; remaining active; maintaining relationships with old and new friends and family; having a sense of humour

Why in a long-term care home: Support required due to her Parkinson's disease, heart ailment, limited vocal communication, inability to walk, and respiratory weakness; excellent relationships with management and residents

Sharon was born in Toronto, Ontario, in 1941 to Lena and Bill. She was an only child until she was six years old, when her sister, Lynda, arrived. The family lived on the third floor in a cold-water flat at Gerrard and Logan. Her mother was a psychiatric nurse at the Queen Street Mental Health Centre (currently the Centre for Addiction and Mental Health, or CAMH) and her father was a sign painter for White Rose Nurseries.

Sharon attended Pape Avenue Public School and Earl Grey Middle School from grades 7 through 10, where she studied typing and shorthand. Sharon was always intrigued by theatre and the arts, and this passion began when she attended the Simpson Avenue United Church where she was involved with a Gilbert and Sullivan theatre group.

Sharon said her extended family came from the area around Belleville, Ontario, more than two hundred years ago. Sharon was very close to her family.

After graduating school, Sharon began working as a secretary. She did marry, but they had no children. When her husband left her in 1963 she was forced to re-evaluate her life. She continued to work as a secretary while she adapted to the changes that life had presented to her.

In 1968, she moved to Calgary, Alberta, and got a job singing for Ernie Castle, and at that time she decided to give up her secretarial work. Sharon worked as a singer for five years and was very good at it (she has videotapes of her singing). She was based in Calgary but travelled all over the West Coast and the Prairies singing in nightclubs while people danced.

After five years she played in *The Prisoner of Second Avenue*, a Neil Simon play at the Theatre Calgary. She also played in the Three Penny Opera in Calgary. She moved back to Toronto in 1976 and got a job in Charlottetown, P.E.I., for a few months. She then travelled to Windsor for the plays *By George* and the *Legend of the Dumbbells*.

During the 1980s in Toronto and environs, she played in theatres such as the Trent Theater, Theatre Passe Muraille, the St. Lawrence Centre for the Arts, and the Muskoka Festival.

Sharon was diagnosed with Parkinson's disease in 1984 but continued to work on the CBC series *9B* until 1990. In 1994, Sharon became a playwright. Sharon worked until 1997, but the disease was progressing. She did two films in 1997: *My Own Country* and *We the Jury*.

The one area Sharon did not talk about was a belief in a higher power. When I asked Sharon if God or spirituality helped her with her numerous difficulties, she responded by saying, "I don't subscribe to any religious or philosophical group. I guess I just have a very strong belief in myself."

She continued, "I have been a fighter all my life. I've had to be. There were many things to fight for — being a fat girl growing up in a thin world. Being an actress, once again a fat one in a thin theatrical world. But I succeeded. I played Auntie Mame in the musical *Mame* for two months in Thunder Bay, the prostitute in *Cabaret* at the St. Lawrence Centre in Toronto, the mother in *Brighton Beach Memoirs* in the Muskoka Festival, and a second production in Sudbury in *O.D. on Paradise*, one of the most successful plays produced by Theatre Passe Muraille. I sang in nightclubs across the country and became a writer at the age of forty. I have starred in and produced a one-woman play called *Sweet Marie* about one of Canada's great actresses, Academy Award winner Marie Dressler.

"I have travelled all over Canada, played every province except for Newfoundland, Yukon Territory, and Nunavut. I was an avid skier and biker (no, not one of those ones, a nice one!). I have been and still am a photographer, I paint, do embroidery, knit and crochet, and before I started writing I read a lot. It has been a life of solitude, but a good life, and I'm glad I lived it. Although I would love to be closer to my sister and my [two] nieces and [two] great-nephews, but they have their lives and careers.

"What I had to face is far too much illness. I was diagnosed in August of 1984 with young-onset Parkinson's disease, so I took off for a few months and spent some time thinking about things. I could have settled down and been comfortable, but I chose to fight it. So I carried on with my career. But it was difficult: I tired easily, so I couldn't go to a lot of opening parties and that was a drag; my balance was affected, [and] I would choreograph my movements on stage to keep from falling. But I would not have traded it for anything. I just wish I could have continued performing longer.

"In 1998 I had an allergic reaction to one of my Parkinson's drugs and ended up with a heart condition. I was in hospital more than twenty-two weeks and came out needing home care. By now, I was living at Performing Arts Lodge. I was one of the first tenants. Many famous people have passed through the doors at PAL: Maureen Forrester, Judith Merril, and Colin Fox. PAL gave me a whole new showbiz family and something to think about. They called me the Cruise Director on the Good Ship PAL. I was president of the Residents' Association. I was director on the PAL Board, ran potluck suppers, and my barbecues on the roof are legendary. I served as treasurer for the St. Lawrence Neighbourhood Association and helped them run their annual picnic. Then last but not least I organized the highly successful Tenth Anniversary Party for PAL.

"Shortly after that the fighter really comes on stage. On Christmas Eve 2003 I had a small accident on the street in my scooter. Paramedics came and took me to the hospital. While in triage, I fell into a coma and didn't wake up until January 30, 2004, thirty-six days later, with my sister standing over me saying, 'You've been gone for a while.' I was left with some souvenirs: respiratory weakness, an inability to walk, and no voice, which is a kick in the head for a singer. But as I said, I did survive.

"Then in January 2007, I had two small strokes. I couldn't fight it anymore and moved in to a nursing home, having to learn a whole new way of life. I share my room with another person. But my name is on a number of lists for homes with private rooms.

"Everyone is nice here, and the facilities are great. I have an excellent relationship with the management and I have lots of new friends and old friends, some who are especially close. There is also my family.

"I have lost sixty pounds, my hair is shiny, and my complexion is clear. I sleep well (nine hours a night), and I used to have insomnia, but no more! I used to think of myself as plain, but hey, I'm not bad looking.

"I miss my friends at PAL, and whenever I go back they welcome me with open arms.

"My boyfriend … calls me his hottie. And he must be right, because one day a delivery man was standing at the elevator reading a poster about me the staff put up about me. It was an outline of my accomplishments. You know what? He called me a hottie too!"

Profile 25

~

NATALIE GUZIK

Natalie Guzik in her room at Stirling Heights Long Term Care Centre, Cambridge, Ontario.
She is writing as she is unable to speak.

Natalie Guzik

High school graduate, office administrator, housewife, painter, volunteer in nursing home, advocate, mother, grandmother, great-grandmother.

Born: Konin, Poland, 1927
Home: Stirling Heights Long Term Care Centre, Cambridge, Ontario

RECEIVING THE HELP I NEED

"While living in a long-term care home, I receive the help I need, I feel safe and secure and I do not have to be a burden on my children. They see me on a regular basis but my health needs are being met by the staff. Due to my speech impairment, I communicate with the help of a computer, pencil and note pad. Once I was shy, but no longer. I have become an advocate in my later years. I am the President of the Residents' Council and have attended meetings at my MPP's office, offering suggestions about what needs to be improved."

I believe it is important to:

- "Recognize that life is what you make it"
- "Treat everyone the same, as we all have much in common"
- "Believe in God"
- "Always stay involved and try to help others"
- "Enjoy activities"

October 2007

History: Office administrator, housewife, painter, volunteer in long-term care home, mother, grandmother, great-grandmother

Born: Konin, Poland, 1927

Currently resident in: Stirling Heights Long Term Care Centre, Cambridge

Keys to enjoying her current years: Support from her family; making new friends; continuing to learn; painting; exercising; learning to cope; not feeling sorry for herself; believing in God

Why in a long-term care home: Physical and emotional support; personal care and assistance from the staff due to her mobility and speech impairments; the comfort of feeling safe; being in a familiar environment

Natalie's parents' names were Walter and Josephine. She had no siblings. In 1928, her father left Poland and came to Canada because he could foresee only wars and domination of his country by other nations such as Russia. He got a job with the Canadian Pacific Railway in Broadview, Saskatchewan, and then sent for the family when Natalie was three years old. She lived in Saskatchewan during the Depression.

"We had a very large garden and grew our own vegetables," she says. "We had a cow and chicken since we lived on the edge of town. During this time, hundreds of men rode the freight trains [as hobos], which slowed down a half mile from town. When the men got off, most of them came to our door, not all at one time, to ask for food, which they always received. We never turned anyone away. The weather was so severe, very cold in the winter, 40 degrees below zero was average and lots of snow. The summers were hot and dry. My mother's health suffered as a result of the weather, so we moved in 1942 to Brantford, Ontario, where I did grades ten to twelve." When Natalie finished high school, she worked at Eaton's for two years. This was around 1947.

After she had worked at Confederation Life for six years, she became the office administrator. She was in her twenties. She met her husband, John Guzik, while she was working at Confederation Life. He worked for thirty-eight years as an industrial engineer for Dominion Rubber, which later became Uniroyal. Before he met Natalie he had been in the Royal Canadian Air Force during the Second World War.

Natalie and John had four children (Richard, Donald, Linda, and Lawrence). Natalie became a full-time housewife after the children were born. The family lived in Kitchener, Ontario, when the children were growing up. Now two children live in Kitchener, one in Fergus, and one in New Brunswick.

John died in 2001 while they were still living in their own home. Natalie lived on her own for a year until August 2002. During this time she could still walk a short distance with her walker, and she had homemakers to help. She then suffered cerebellum syndrome, which caused her to lose her balance and her speech. This was the precipitating factor that caused her to move to a long-term care home.

Natalie said that she could have remained at home for a few more months, but she needed some help. Now she has assistance when going to the bathroom. She said that she has now graduated to a mechanical lift. The staff provide personal care and assistance with her bathing.

Natalie has found meaning while living in a long-term care home by writing letters, painting, reading, and learning to use a computer — a gift from her family. It is difficult for Natalie to speak due to the cerebellum syndrome, but she has not let this hold her back from being creative and communicating with people. When she was being interviewed for this project she used a pen and paper to communicate her thoughts.

When asked how she exercises her body and her mind she said that the staff encourages her to get up, and she goes to exercise classes twice a week. She also reads, plays Scrabble and solitaire, listens to the radio, watches television, and works on her computer.

Faith in God has helped her with her difficulties and throughout life; so too have her loving family and friends. She inherited her father's sense of humour. "I was never a leader, always shy, but I could talk non-stop," she recalls.

Her business affairs are in order, her burial arrangements are paid for, and her will is made out, and Natalie feels a sense of relief to have all of this looked after.

These are the words of wisdom Natalie has for others: try to love one another; have faith in God, prayer, family, friends, and people; be kind to people; don't put things off; and life is what happens when you are busy making other plans.

She has been secretary of the Residents' Council since it started at her long-term care home and also treasurer-secretary at food committee meetings. She helps at fundraisers, for example for the Alzheimer's Society, despite her inability to communicate verbally. She has been active in this role since moving to Stirling Heights.

"It all started with the need for more staff here," Natalie said. "Obviously, someone with my family's history of helping out during the Depression is still keenly aware of the need to help when it was necessary. As an advocate, I have attended each and every meeting at my MPP's office [as part of a group representing the residents of Stirling Heights] and written letters to both my MPP and to the Minister of Health and Long-Term Care demanding additional funding for care and services in nursing homes. I have also been active in signing petitions and recruiting signatures. I have openly shared my comments and suggestions about what needs to be improved in the nursing care system with my MPP. I am no longer shy!"

Natalie likes to keep busy; her husband taught her not to feel sorry for herself, and when she sees others in pain and more handicapped she stops feeling any self-pity.

Part II

ARTICLES AND TOOLS

MUSIC AND DEMENTIA

When I was working as a social worker at Providence Centre, a long-term care health care facility and long-term care home in Toronto, I wondered what I could do to communicate with the residents who had dementia and advanced Alzheimer's disease. I decided that on Friday afternoons, when there was some free time, I would start a music appreciation group for residents who were quite impaired and did not leave the floor. I purchased a cassette player and a few cassettes and found a volunteer who was willing to assist with locating appropriate music, setting up the chairs, and bringing the residents to the group.

Having read a book entitled *Music and the Mind* by Anthony Storr, I became inspired. He claims, "Although we live in a strongly visual and verbal culture, the sense with the most direct route to the emotions is hearing." I discovered that there were people in the room who could not remember where their room was and if they had had lunch that day but who knew every word to the songs that I played because they had been familiar with them in their early years. Their long-term memory could still be reached. When the songs were played they were living in the moment and their passion for living returned: if only for a short time they were joyous and with me.

Not all of the people had a form of dementia or Alzheimer's disease; some were frail and suffering from other diseases such as Huntington's disease, Parkinson's disease, multiple sclerosis, and Korsakov's psychosis. While working with this varied group, I discovered the beauty of music. "Music is perhaps one of the few media through which such compromises can be achieved, in that music can be enjoyed at different levels at the same time by different members of a group."[1]

I chose music that the residents would have been familiar with when they were in the early to middle

1. Anthony Storr, *Music and the Mind* (New York: Macmillan, Inc., 1992), 22.

years of their adult lives. "Music-based therapy is using old memory traces which are intact and we can therefore often reach those who are otherwise inaccessible."[2]

I experienced things that I carry with me to this day. A husband and wife, Mr. and Mrs. G., were living at Providence. Mr. G. was suffering from Parkinson's disease and rarely spoke. His wife asked if we could bring a copy of "O sole mio," a beautiful opera song that Mr. G. had loved throughout his life. When I played the song, he immediately smiled and tears welled up in his eyes. He turned to his wife and sang the song in a beautiful

voice, as he had been a very good singer in his younger years. Everyone in the room was touched, and I still remember the awe of that special moment.

In the photograph in this piece, I show Helen Stewart, a singer who travels to various long-term care homes singing to seniors and other residents who live there. Her company is called Melody Magic. She has experienced similar moments of awe.

"While three or four of the residents were singing along, I noticed one man who was looking at me with a look of bewilderment. He wasn't singing or clapping and didn't seem to be responding to me in any way. He

2. Storr, *Music and the Mind*, 22.

Helen Stewart singing to a group of cognitively impaired seniors at the Rekai Centre, Toronto, Ontario.

was just staring into space," she recalls. Helen said that she tries to remember that some of these folks may be unable to respond.

"I strolled over to him, touched his shoulder, and asked him carefully if he liked the songs. There was a very slight nod of the head and a twinkling lost look in his eye. I then responded by saying, 'How about Elvis Presley, do you like his songs?' Almost immediately his lips started to move and a small sound came out as he sang the song with me.

"The nurses started to talk to each other and took notice of what was happening. Others came down the hall to look. The nurses all looked completely stunned and shocked as they watched and didn't take their eyes off of him. After that I went directly into another Elvis Presley song, 'Don't Be Cruel.' And he continued to sing ever so softly the entire song. He hadn't spoken in two years."

Music helps build bridges with people who hear it, even if it is temporary. While they hear the music residents' wandering and aggression can be reduced and social interaction and attention to surroundings can be increased. "We can hope to provide a means of enjoyment and personal satisfaction, to counteract at least some of the sadness, and to maintain some sense of creativity and fun, which is usually lacking in institutional life."[3] Music can build up self-esteem in the residents, give them a sense of achievement and success, and help them communicate their feelings, hopes, and fears; it can give a sense of individuality to those whom the world tends to write off as worthless.

How the room is arranged can affect the residents' experience. Often a circle is the best choice rather than

rows. They will gain stimulation by seeing other people joining in with the music, and they may be more inclined to participate.

Music, possibly even religious music, is also important when counselling dying patients as music can help them say the final things that need to be said. Through our musical intervention at the bedside we may be able to help the family to feel that they are involved in those last days of care and help them cope with the coming separation. The care of the dying is always a challenge to our empathy and to our thinking about life and death, and working with a dying person who is also suffering dementia provides us with a double challenge. Through the empathic use of music, it may be possible to meet those challenges and give to both patient and family a sense of being understood and comforted in a way which is otherwise unavailable. The healing power of music is powerful and quite amazing.

Helen Stewart shares the story of a wonderful breakthrough at Seven Oaks. "I'm just the strolling musician and don't know what the patients are actually suffering, but I do know that on the second floor, the folks are mostly despondent or in a world of their own with some form of dementia," she says.

"On one particular Sunday while making my rounds I saw a familiar face enter the room with a skip in her step, a woman who normally smiles and mutters to herself. She walked directly towards me, singing with me in a beautiful voice. I complimented her and asked her to keep singing. I quickly searched my mind for old familiar songs that she would know. Sure enough she continued to sing with me.

"Two nurses joined us standing in the middle of the room. They had expressions of amazement on their

3. Ruth Bright, *Music Therapy and the Dementias: Improving the Quality of Life* (St. Louis: MMB Music Inc.), vi.

faces. We all found a seat close by and continued to talk and sing with the patient. Fighting back tears, the woman said, 'If only my mother could see me now.' She continued to tell us how her mother taught the songs to her and how she was so good to her and her siblings.

"One nurse was standing in front of us with her hand to her mouth, also fighting back tears. The other nurse sat beside her and encouraged conversation. I pulled out another song, 'Oh Susanna.' The woman sang every word, and as she held the melody I jumped to a harmony part and we had a perfect duet. It was amazing.

"She continued to tell stories, and I learned that she was a French-speaking woman from Quebec. I attempted to sing the French song, and she helped me with the lyrics. Did you ever see the movie *The Notebook* where in the end the woman comes right back from her dementia for short periods of time? It was just like that. It was another extraordinary day in my attempts to reach these wonderful people.

"Music exalts life, enhances life and gives it meaning. Great music outlives the individual who created it. It is both personal and beyond the personal. For those who love it, it remains as a fixed point of reference in an unpredictable world. Music is a source of reconciliation, exhilaration and hope which never fails."

HOLY BLOSSOM SENIORS GROUP

I went out to Holy Blossom Temple, a reform synagogue in Toronto, to speak to a seniors group about what we can all do to protect our fragile environment. Rosemary Frei, a freelance writer and journalist and a nominated candidate for the Green Party, presented with me.

As I had a typical group of seniors (around thirty men and women) I decided to take the opportunity to ask them what they saw as the positives and negatives of life in a long-term care home. All of these men and women were still living in their own homes. This is the feedback that I received.

Positive Feedback

One person said that he knew of a cardiologist whose doctor told him that he would not live for very long if he did not lose some weight. He had just moved into a long-term care home, and with the help of the staff there he lost thirty pounds. His health and his life have improved and he is doing very well.

Another person said that most people that she knows who now live in long-term care homes have family and friends visit quite frequently. Plus they have a built-in community around them in addition to their family and friends.

The group talked about the fact that by being in a long-term care home they are not isolated at home with a caregiver. That can be boring when there is just you and the caregiver and there is not a lot to do but watch television, which is often depressing. The conversations become stagnant.

They said that while living in a long-term care home there are numerous new programs and you can be entertained by the other residents. People come from all over the world and from different religious backgrounds, and you can learn other customs and hear new stories. They felt it would be interesting hearing about the experiences other people had acquired over long lifetimes. They said that they were thankful to be able to go into a place of their choice.

They also said that they had concerns that sometimes a caregiver would fall asleep at night while they were living in their own homes, but when living in a long-term care home there is always a night shift to call if necessary.

Negative Feedback

Some of the negatives that were discussed included concerns that they would all be treated the same and not according to individual requirements. They felt that there would not be a distinction between alert and drugged or cognitively impaired people. Many never got up early while living in their own homes and now they would have to get up when everyone else did. They also said that if you have to have a caregiver you may as well remain in familiar surroundings and in a larger room.

Conclusions

Each person, with the help of his or her family or friends, needs to visit several long-term care homes before thinking about that option. People may even choose to stay over at a facility for a few days to see if a long-term care home is the right option. They can also talk to others who may be in a long-term care home.

Moving into a long-term care home is not an easy decision, but it may be the right one when it becomes necessary to have more care than can be provided while living in your own home.

Facing the end of life is never an easy situation, whether living in your own home or in a long-term care home. No one wants to grow old and feeble and lose their independence, and most do not want to face the end of life, but we will all have to face these issues and it may be best to do so in a long-term care home where support and counselling are provided.

Staying at home may be better for some, but not for everyone: much depends on resources and support from family and or community.

DEBBY VIGODA'S STORY

June 1, 2003, is indelibly etched in our family's memory.

On that sunny June afternoon, my husband, Morris, and I were searching for a special shirt for a special jacket at one of the men's clothing stores in downtown Toronto. One moment we were busy checking out the advantages of one shirt over another, and a few moments later our lives were changed dramatically. Quite unexpectedly, my husband fainted and hit his head on the slate floor. An ambulance arrived within minutes, by which time Morris had regained consciousness. The attendants checked him over, and although they found the back of his head to be bleeding, his vital signs seemed normal. Morris was able to respond appropriately to questions asked by the paramedics, who recommended strongly that he be taken to the nearest hospital, where a number of tests were ordered. All appeared normal for a few hours — and then the damage began to appear. The severity of the impact onto the slate floor had not only caused a skull fracture but had resulted in Morris's brain being thrown against his skull, leading to brain swelling and internal bleeding. For almost a month we did not know if this healthy, active man of eighty-five would survive this terrible accident. And once he rallied, we did not know whether he would be bedridden or wheelchair-bound, or whether he would ever walk or talk, or eat normally, or even be able to think and reason.

The accident had happened in the middle of the SARS outbreak, and so I was unable to spend much time with Morris in the hospital. When I was allowed to visit, I was swathed in gown, cap, goggles, masks, and gloves. Questions swirled in my mind about the kind of care I would be able to give him, if and when he recovered.

Like many families today, our children are thousands of miles away: our son is on the other side of the country, our daughter in the middle of Africa. But they responded immediately to the crisis that was facing our family, and in less than twelve hours Alan was by my side, with Marcy arriving in Toronto a few days later. Their support during those early uncertain days, and of course since, was vital. But they did have to return to their families and their work. And so I was dependent on friends and colleagues and on my children's support from afar.

After a month of acute care Morris was transferred to a transitional unit. He was still on oxygen and tube-fed, but was able to be moved into a wheelchair for a short while and to slowly attempt to take a few steps, holding on to the tall walker. At this point, friends were able to take a role in helping him recover his speech and cognition.

At the end of the second month in the acute hospital, he was transferred to a rehabilitation hospital. During the two months of rehabilitation, the focus was on the normal activities of daily living. He slowly began to learn to walk, to swallow, and to eat. He gradually learned how to complete the tasks that we take so for granted — selecting his clothes for the day, washing and dressing himself, and deciding which food choice he would prefer.

Three months after that eventful afternoon, the full rehabilitation team completed a home assessment. It was obvious that Morris required twenty-four-hour, seven-day-a-week care and security because of his limited physical and mental abilities. And so there was recognition that a care home was needed.

How did we determine what the appropriate setting was for Morris? We were fortunate that for thirty-five years I had been working with the elderly and with staff who work with older adults. As an educator with a special focus in gerontology, I was knowledgeable about many of the circumstances that older adults face. As the

executive director of the Ontario Gerontology Association, with its office in a long-term care home, I had a network of colleagues whom I called upon to help me as I worked through many of the issues that were presented to us while Morris was in the hospitals. Four months after the accident, Morris became a resident of one of Toronto's homes.

During the eleven years that I had my OGA office in a long-term care home, the office was on the same floor as the secured unit for those residents who needed additional supervision and support. When we were first there, residents in the unit would constantly be rattling the door, to attempt to open it. Over the years, with the new developments in care of residents with various forms of dementia, I noted the residents became significantly calmer, and when I visit the unit most of them are engrossed in one activity or another.

Over the years, as our life situations change, there are adjustments to be made. If we go off to school and leave our parents' home, we have to learn to do things differently. When we marry or go into a relationship, there are necessary changes, compromises, and changes of priority. Think of the kind of adjustments that are made by people who move for their jobs. And so we had to recognize that there *were* adjustments to be made when Morris moved from our home and the hospital into a long-term care home.

Morris and I certainly had many adjustments to make. The biggest, after forty-five years of marriage, was not being together almost all the time. Most of the adjustments were those that *he* had to make. To accept that other people would be looking after his physical needs. Eating different foods than he had been used to. Having to adjust to a very different schedule.

Life in a long-term care home *is* very different from the life that one leads in one's own residence, whether it be large or small, whether it be a room, an apartment, or a house. We really don't think about the number of people who attend to the needs of residents in a care home. Morris and I often talk about the fact that more than twenty people look after his needs every day: there are the registered nurses, the personal support aides, the housekeeping and maintenance staff, the cooks and servers, the therapists and recreationists, the laundry and dietary staff, and the volunteers, as well as the doctors, the pharmacists, and the other health professionals who see residents on a less frequent basis. Each has an impact on the care of and quality of life for each person in a home. When I think of Morris's needs on a day-to-day basis — let alone in an emergency — and recognize the strength of the team, I become even more aware of my own physical and psychological limitations; I am only one person, whose major skill in an emergency is the ability to call 911!

After Morris was discharged from the hospital and was admitted to the long-term care home, he was very unhappy. He was convinced that I did not want him at home, even though it was dangerous for him to be at our house. When we would go out for an afternoon or for lunch or dinner, he would make derogatory remarks about the care home, which made me even more unhappy.

From the moment that the family knew that Morris would survive and would need extensive care, we knew that we had to focus on my needs and recognize my limitations. I would do Morris no good — and would in fact be a detriment to his recovery — if I burned out. How was I going to take care of *me* so that I could take care of my husband? We are well aware of caregiver burn-out and the toll it takes on both the caregiver and the care recipient. What I had to concentrate on was helping enhance his quality of life, not through being the hands-on caregiver but rather by enhancing the care he received in a long-term care home.

I also realized how little we are conscious of the hazards that exist where we live, and how long-term care homes, by definition, are highly aware of those areas that might create risks to safety. We don't think about the extension cords or chairs or tables that might tip. We ignore unsafe surfaces. Staff in care homes are constantly on the watch.

And what can be said for the importance of companionship. We don't think about how lonely it can be in one's own home, even if there is a partner or a companion. And all the more so if there is no one else present. Of course, no one is going to like everyone else in a care home. There are few people who like everyone they meet. But there are opportunities to develop friendships through roommates and tablemates, through joining in activities of the home, through going on bus trips and sitting in the garden, through becoming friends with staff and volunteers. The opportunities for developing relationships are endless and are there for the taking.

If we were to list all of the activities that go on in a long-term care home over the course of a month, we would be overwhelmed by the range of options. There are special breakfasts and dinners, there are holiday and birthday celebrations throughout the year, and sometimes there are newly created celebrations like the first day of spring. There are the endless choices of card and board games; there is a multiplicity of craft options; there are exercise programs ranging from simple chair exercises to more rigorous ones; there are outings for special meals, coffee, changing of the leaves, Christmas lights, botanical gardens, shopping, and more. Entertainment is provided regularly on the floors by volunteers of all ages who come to sing, dance, and entertain for all those who wish to join them. There are committees that residents can join, including food committees and residents' councils. The spiritual and religious needs of residents are addressed in a variety of ways through volunteer and paid clergy at services and special cultural events. The choices are many!

There are residents who have no family or who may be estranged from family, or who have few friends. But for those who have family and friends, these connections are important and help to enrich residents' lives.

How do I help to enhance the quality of life for my husband? When I can, I join him on some of the outings. I have dinner with him and his tablemates on occasion. We go down to Coffee House on Wednesday evenings. I help arrange for him to join friends for lunch every few weeks. We go to concerts together during the year, and we go out for dinner a few times a month. And I am with him for a few hours each day, if I am in town and well.

Morris is resigned to the reality of his life. He naturally would prefer to be at home, but he recognizes that he could not be properly cared for. So he takes part in some of the activities of the home, goes to the occasional meeting, enjoys visits from friends, and looks forward to mail, pictures, phone calls, and visits from our children.

Of course, we would prefer if life had *not* changed on June 1, 2003. But it did, and we are making the most of what we have together at the home and in the community. Morris has an enhanced life supported by a caring team.

THE CHANGING SHAPE OF
OUR FAMILY AND ELDERCARE NEEDS

BY PATRICIA MOFFAT

In this book Irene's photographs challenge the prevailing image of aging and long-term care. We are inspired by the wisdom and creativity of some of our elders living in long-term care homes. Family caregivers us tell about their journeys and their points of view. The family and our eldercare needs are changing, but we can influence how problems are defined and how policies are developed in the future.

My lifelong journey in social work began with the influence of my grandfather. He was born in 1870, lived in our home through my teenage years, and died at a soccer game at age eighty-three. His long life in municipal politics and public service was informed by the values and the economic realities of the nineteenth century. He saw and welcomed many changes in society, and he taught me optimism, saying "It's a poor heart that never rejoices."

In my forty years as a social worker in Ontario I have seen changes too: in public policy, in the workplace, and in the shape of the family whose caregivers are an integral part of the care provided in any long-term care home. I plan to review some of these changes, then present some ideas and observations that sustain the optimism my grandfather taught me all those years ago.

In 1981, when I began to work with seniors at the Baycrest Centre for Geriatric Care in Toronto, I had already heard Elaine Brody's term "the sandwich generation": middle-aged working people, most of them women, caught between the needs of their careers, their growing children, and their frail elderly parents. In 1982, Walter Lyons asked me to edit the proceedings of the Social Work Clinic Day about Baycrest's Adult Day Care program. In it, social worker Anna VanDelman shared the protest of a seventy-year-old son, arriving to pick up his father, who had been taken ill at day care: "He's in better shape than I am!" Anna's client was driven home by his mid-life grandson, with two generations of elders in the back seat. Today, it is not uncommon to have two generations of seniors in a family, with daughters and sons in their seventies caring for parents in their nineties and early one hundreds.

The mobility of our families is another factor, with Vancouver elders whose adult children and grandchildren are in Toronto or Texas. Young families are adopting elderly friends to be grandparents to their children because their own parents and grandparents live far away. The kinship networks of blood that bound people together in the past are being replaced by networks born of proximity, shared beliefs and values, and common interests. All the more reason for long-term care homes and eldercare agencies to reach out to schools and community groups nearby so that new intergenerational bonds can be forged, connecting children to the past and elders to the younger generation. In this way traditions can be maintained, stories told, and skills shared that would otherwise be lost.

In 1991, when I was social work team leader for Medicine and Oncology at Sunnybrook Health Sciences Centre, Noreen Kay and I wrote a paper called "The New Patient Mix." In it we observed first that people over eighty-five were the fastest growing group of elders, many of them surviving for years in long-term care homes and hospitals, and second that elderly people needing health care support in the community were often poorly served by a hospital-based system geared to acute and episodic care. We illustrated how mutual support and educational groups can enhance continuity of care for elderly patients and their family caregivers.

At present, the fastest growing age group in our society is people aged fifty-six to sixty-four, so we have a second chance to change the system. In the years since

Brody told us about the sandwich generation, more women are in the workforce with later childbearing and extended years of care and support for the children they do have. At the most demanding stage of their careers, many of these women face the retirement of their spouses, not always in the best of health, along with an increased need to give support to their elderly parents.

But we are also seeing positive and creative responses to some of these changes. People of all ages are seeking a better work/family balance, and a lot of small and home-based businesses are being started, many of them by women seeking to combine paid employment with volunteer, family, and community interests. In the competition to recruit and retain skilled workers, more companies are adding new benefits, including compassionate leave, flexible hours, and eldercare consultation services. In his book *Prime Time*, Marc Freedman called America's healthy aging population "the country's only increasing natural resource."

Also remarkable is the increase in intergenerational projects (local, regional, and international) joining young and old to build affordable housing, develop artistic skills, welcome newcomers, and provide needed care to frail and vulnerable individuals. As executive director of the Centre for Intergenerational Learning at Temple University in Philadelphia, Dr. Nancy Henkin has been promoting and demonstrating policies that would build "communities for all ages." The centre is challenging the provision of "silo funding" that can lead to the segregation of the young from their elders, when they can learn from and give so much to one another. Their Web site is www.comingofage.org.

In his 1982 book *Humanizing Institutions for the Aged*, Lee. H. Bowker argued that the main characteristic of a successful long-term care or retirement home is its permeability. He observed that the quality of life of residents improved in proportion to any increase of traffic (whether people, ideas, or activities) between the facility and people of all ages in the community that surrounded it. Surely such traffic could only improve the quality of support available to family caregivers of the residents too.

All of this is a work in progress, and I live in hope that my comments will soon be out of date. Recent policy initiatives in support of home-based health care are reason enough for optimism, but these policies need vocal and active support to ensure that they are implemented and sustained. As people become better informed and more involved in the issues that affect them and their family members, the pressure for such changes can only increase, to the future benefit of our elders and the society they worked so hard to build.

SPEECH FOR THE OFFICIAL EXHIBIT OPENING

BY MAUREEN HUTCHINSON

This speech was written by Maureen Hutchinson to be given at the official launch of the photography and text exhibit "Aging is Living: A New Perspective" on April 30, 2008, on the top floor of the G. Raymond Chang School of Continuing Education at Ryerson University, Heaslip House, Toronto. Due to unforeseen circumstances, Maureen could not deliver the speech, so it is set out here.

Old age is a great gift, and there is a great freedom that comes with aging. As you get older, it is easier to be positive: you care less about what people think and you have earned the right to your own opinion. I love being old. I like the person I have become and the new interests I have developed as a resident of West Park Healthcare Centre during the past six years. As president of the Residents' Council there and as president of the Ontario Association of Residents' Councils,

and through my involvement with MOHLTC [Ministry of Health and Long-Term Care] and TC/LHIN [Toronto Central Local Health Integrated Network], I am well occupied daily with both internal and external responsibilities related to residents' interests and developments in health care, but I also have time for some more personal pursuits like reading and socializing. Life is a continuous learning process, and as we grow older we can enjoy the rewarding experience of learning new ideas and sharing our past with others in the community. Four years ago I was introduced, through a few lessons by recreation staff, to the joys of word processing and Internet access; I bought my own computer and now spend many happy hours contacting friends via e-mail, researching, and typing the centre's quarterly newsletter. Very quickly a whole new world opened for me. Many retirees like having the time to pursue their current hobbies or some other interests — perhaps woodwork, needlepoint, art, or music — for which there was no time during a busy career. Many residents in long-term care have talents that they continue to use and that they generously share with others: many learn new skills and gain confidence from their mentors' example. It is not the years in your life that count; it is the life in your years. Keep active. Keep alert. Keep alive. Recently I saw a cartoon that very aptly describes the situation in any long-term care residence: "Crayons are all different colours and often have funny names, but they all live together in the one box."

TWENTY-ONE KEY POINTS ABOUT PEOPLE WHO HAVE AGED WITH A HEALTHY ATTITUDE

This list was created by combining information from my first book, Treasured Legacies: Older & Still Great, *with perspective gained from interviewing the twenty-five people in this book.*

People who age well …

1) often have a sense of wonder when looking at the world; they still see the beauty and awe that nature holds for us.

2) have a positive attitude despite the difficulties that life inevitably presents to all as they grow older: problems are not seen as something that will defeat them but rather as challenges to resolve and overcome or to live with if the problem cannot be solved.

3) are connected to family, friends, and their community (the term *community* varies greatly; a community can be a place of worship, a seniors' centre, a college where they learn or participate, a hiking club …).

4) realize the greatest happiness is not achieved by acquiring more material possessions but comes from being kind, giving back, having family and friends, and being of service to the community.

5) have love in their lives, whether from a child, grandchild, spouse, pet, or friend.

6) reach out and give to others: they are compassionate, they are not self-centred, they focus on the world around them, and they are able to go beyond just thinking about themselves.

7) keep growing their entire lives; they believe in life-long learning, there may be a new interest they have always wanted to discover and now at the latter part of their lives they have the time to pursue new interests such as learning to use computers, writing their memoirs, or whatever it is that will help fulfill their lives.

8) are passionate about something or many things; passion is such an important part of aging well.

9) are able to forgive those who have harmed them and they have learned to be more compassionate by learning to forgive.

10) often do some kind of volunteer work; they use the skills they have acquired over a lifetime and act as consultants or mentors to teach younger people.

11) have developed friendships with people of all ages as they have grown older and as friends begin to pass away, they are less likely to be left alone at the end of their lives.

12) have a sense of humour and can laugh at themselves and at life in general.

13) have come to accept their impending death and see it as a natural progression of life.

14) are religious or spiritual or both; of all the people I interviewed 80 percent said religion or spirituality or both helped them get through difficult times.

15) feel a sense of serenity and gratitude as they grow older.

16) are concerned about the legacy they will leave behind and want to leave the world a better place after they are gone.

17) want to make each day count; the Buddhist philosophy is to be aware of one's impending death and life's finite nature every day so that each day is lived with purpose, meaning, and intent.

18) have come to accept their limitations and weaknesses and are leading rich, full lives despite their human frailties.

19) believe in doing everything in moderation.

20) are able to adapt to the changes in their own lives and see the changes as a normal part of the aging process; they have also become more flexible as part of being less rigid in that they accept those changes happening in today's world such as couples living together before they marry, interracial marriages, same-sex marriages, etc.

21) *exercise* — exercise their minds and their bodies, build exercise into their daily routines, climb stairs, forget the car, and walk according to their abilities and according to what their physical limitations allow, read, talk, share experiences, learn how to use computers, etc.

In conclusion, seniors who are aging well have a greater historical perspective, and there were common threads that linked all these people together despite differences in gender, race, culture, and socioeconomic and religious backgrounds. They were less judgmental and showed an acceptance and tolerance of differences in people. They were kinder, more compassionate, and less prejudiced. They possessed a more universalistic approach towards life. These ideals have helped these seniors fare better in the aging process. These elders are wise and are a source of inspiration to succeeding generations.

"IF I DON'T TAKE CARE OF ME, I CAN'T TAKE CARE OF HIM"
A CAREGIVER'S CHECKLIST

BY DEBBY VIGODA

If you are taking care of a loved one, be it a family member or friend, you must take care of yourself. Most caregivers are very devoted to the person they are caring for. Try to start each day on a positive note, which should include laughter — joy and laughter affect the way you feel about caregiving, and thus the way it is done.

Regardless of the reason for or extent of the caregiving you provide, you are trying to do the best you can. Remember that it can be physically and emotionally stressful for everyone concerned, and the caregiver burden could result in burnout. "Burnout" is defined as a state of physical, emotional, and psychological exhaustion, frequently accompanied by a change in attitude from positive and caring to negative and uncaring.

You are not alone! There are thousands of people across the country that understand your problems and are willing to help. There are innumerable resources that we can access. There are health and social service professionals, family members, friends, community agencies, books, and websites, some or all of which can provide support and information. For some people, caregiving provides a rewarding spiritual journey.

The following is a short list to help you help yourself.

Information

- Do you have the information that you need to be an effective caregiver?
- Do you have a sufficient understanding of the health status of the care receiver, in order to provide appropriate care?
- Are you the best person to get the information that you need, or is there someone else who could get the information and ease your load?

- Do you have contact with a community agency that would provide support services for the care receiver and for you?
- If it is appropriate, are you connected with a disease-specific organization, e.g. Parkinson Society Canada, the Canadian Diabetes Association, or the Alzheimer's Society?

Expectations

- Do you have realistic expectations of what you can do for your care receiver and what others are able and willing to do?
- Have you realistically assessed your own capabilities and set appropriate goals?
- Do you have any health problems or limitations that could affect your caregiving?
- Do you have realistic expectations about the success and outcome of your caregiving?

Emotional Strength

- Do you have the emotional strength to cope with the roller coaster of caregiving responsibilities and demands?
- Do you regularly assess the health status and needs of your care receiver?
- What are you doing to ensure that you are mentally and physically fit?
- Do you have feelings of guilt that you are not doing enough or that the caregiver isn't happy?
- Do you have regular respite from your caregiving?

Support Network

- Do you have a support network? (This could be made up of family members; friends; neighbours; your minister, priest, or rabbi; or a support group through an agency or in your house of worship.)
- Do you talk to other caregivers about different approaches to situations and problems?
- Do you ask for help, and if offered help do you not reject it?
- Have you made a life of your own apart from caregiving?

Caregiver Burnout

- Is it possible that you are suffering from caregiver burnout? There are three stages of burnout, which frequently overlap: the first is frustration; the second is depression, and the third is despair.
- Do you know the signs of caregiver burnout?

  - Are you irritable?
  - Are you impatient?
  - Do you feel alienated?
  - Do you feel a lack of compassion?
  - Are you sensitive to criticism?
  - Do you withdraw?
  - Have you lost hope?

- Do you know what to do to prevent burnout?
- Do you know how to deal with burnout?

Cost of Caregiving

- Are you worried about the cost of caregiving?
- Have you had to leave work, diminish your work hours, or dip into your savings, all of which add to the burden of caregiving?

Think of your accomplishments as a caregiver. It is time to acknowledge the successes that you have had! Don't allow yourself to become overwhelmed by the demands of caregiving. No martyrs need apply! Review the checklist and take care of yourself. Give yourself a gold star or a special treat in recognition of a job well done. You deserve it!

CONCERNED FRIENDS CHECKLIST

Following is a long-term care home checklist produced by an Ontario organization called Concerned Friends, with specific references to Ontario facilities and telephone numbers. Although the entire document will be most helpful to residents of Ontario, the checklist will certainly allow anyone in Canada or the United States to check out homes in their area with pertinent questions.

Concerned Friends is a non-profit, volunteer, consumer corporation and registered charity dedicated to reform of the long-term care system and improvement of quality of life for residents.

Concerned Friends of Ontario Citizens
in Care Facilities
140 Merton St., 2nd Floor, Toronto, Ontario
M4S 1A1 (416) 489-0146
Copyright

LONG-TERM CARE HOMES CHECKLIST

The Purpose of this checklist is primarily to assist anyone who is choosing a Long-Term Care Home.

Before assuming that a Long-Term Care Home is the "best place" to be, however, inquire about alternative services such as Home Care, Home Support, and Supportive Housing.

If you do opt for a provincially regulated long-term care home, here are some preliminary steps to take before making a choice:

❑ Obtain a list of homes from your local Community Care Access Centre.

❑ Examine homes closely before agreeing to the admission of oneself, a relative or a friend.

- Resist pressure from either hospitals or the placement coordinator to admit someone to the first available bed. Take the time to thoroughly investigate the options.

- Determine from the Placement Co-ordinator whether a home you are considering is "under enforcement." The Co-ordinator is required to explain this concept to you, as it reflects the current conditions in the facility.

- If you have internet access, you may want to visit Reports on Long-term Care Homes on the Ministry of Health and Long-Term Care website for further information. http://www.health.gov.on.ca.

GENERAL INFORMATION

- Nursing Homes, Municipal Homes and Charitable Homes for the Aged are provincially regulated long-term care homes and are accountable to the Ministry of Health and Long-Term Care. They are regulated under Bill 140, an Act respecting long-term care homes, which was passed in May 2007. This Act sets out both the rights of the residents and the responsibilities of the home and includes provisions for family and resident councils. Copies can be obtained from Publications Ontario, 880 Bay Street, Toronto, Ontario, M7A 1N8. Telephone (416) 326-5300 or toll-free 1-800-668-9938.

- The Ministry of Health and Long-Term Care is responsible for monitoring, evaluating and taking action to ensure that all long-term care homes comply with the applicable acts and regulations, the terms and conditions of the service agreement, the Program Manual, and Ministry policies and directives. The Program Manual sets out the standards and guidelines for the day-to-day operation of the home. Compliance advisors have the primary responsibility for monitoring and evaluating facilities' performance. A resident, family member or advocate who is concerned about the care or conditions in a facility and has been unsuccessful in resolving the problem with the home, should contact the service area office to make a complaint to the Compliance Advisor. Concerned Friends will also try to advise and support anyone having problems in a long-term care facility.

- It is advisable to receive legal advice regarding the Admission Contract to the Long-Term Care home. In particular, check that you are not signing away rights and services that would be covered under Bill 140. You are not at present obligated to sign a contract, because without doing so, the provisions of the Bill apply. Only sign the contract if it ENHANCES your rights, not if it DIMINISHES them.

INITIAL VISIT TO FACILITY

- Meet with the Administrator and, if possible, the Director of Care Planning.

- Obtain written and verbal information about the home using the attached questionnaire (see page 3)

❏ Request copies of:

    1) Admission Contract
    2) Compliance Review Report
    3) Residents' Bill of Rights

❏ Attempt to talk with families of existing residents either in the home or arrange to meet them off the premises for feedback on their experiences and observations.

IMPORTANT PHONE NUMBERS

Ministry of Health and Long-Term Care
General Inquiry 1-800-268-1153 TTY 1-800-387-5559

Long-term Care ACTION Line 1-866-434-0144
(7 days a week, from 8:30 a.m. to 7:00 p.m.)

Contact information for
Local Health Integration Networks

www.lhins.on.ca

LHIN: Erie St. Clair
Address: 180 Riverview Drive, Chatham, ON
    N7M 5Z8
Telephone: 519-351-5677, 1-866-231-5446

LHIN: South West
Address: 201 Queens Avenue, Suite 700, London,
    ON N6A 1J1
Telephone: 519-672-0445, 1-866-294-5446

LHIN: Waterloo Wellington
Address: 55 Wyndham Street North, Suite 212,
    Guelph, ON N1H 7T8
Telephone: 519-822-6208, 1-866-306-5446

LHIN: Hamilton Niagara Haldimand Brant
Address: 270 Main Street East, Units1–6, Grimsby,
    ON L3M 1P8
Telephone: 905-945-4930, 1-866-363-5446

LHIN: Central West
Address: 8 Nelson Street West, Suite 300, Brampton,
    ON L6X 4J2
Telephone: 905-455-1281, 1-866-370-5446

LHIN: Mississauga Halton
Address: 700 Dorval Drive, Suite 500, Oakville, ON
    L6K 3V3
Telephone: 905-337-7131, 1-866-371-5446

LHIN: Toronto Central
Address: 425 Bloor Street East, Suite 201, Toronto,
    ON M4W 3R5
Telephone: 416-921-7453, 1-866-383-5446

LHIN: Central
Address: 140 Allstate Parkway, Suite 210, Markham,
    ON L3R 5Y8
Telephone: 905-948-1872, 1-866-392-5446

LHIN: Central East
Address: Harwood Plaza, 314 Harwood Avenue
    South, Suite 204A, Ajax, ON L1S 2J1
Telephone: 905-427-5497, 1-866-804-5446

LHIN: South East
Address: 48 Dundas Street West, Unit 2, Belleville,
           ON K8P 1A3
Telephone: 613-967-0196, 1-866-831-5446

LHIN: Champlain
Address: 1900 City Park Drive, Suite 204, Ottawa,
           ON K1J 1A3
Telephone: 613-747-6784, 1-866-902-5446

LHIN: North Simcoe Muskoka
Address: 210 Memorial Avenue, Suites 127–130,
           Orillia, ON L3V 7V1
Telephone: 705-326-7750, 1-866-903-5446

LHIN: North East
Address: 555 Oak Street East, 3rd Floor, North Bay,
           ON P1B 8E3
Telephone: 705-840-2872, 1-866-906-5446

LHIN: North West
Address: 975 Alloy Drive, Suite 201, Thunder Bay,
           ON P7B 5Z8
Telephone: 807-684-9425, 1-866-907-5446

Contact Information for the Compliance Management Program

To contact the Compliance Advisor for a home, call the Long-term Care Action Line, or the Service Area Office for your area. The province is divided into five areas as listed below.

LHIN: Erie St. Clair
Area: London
Phone Number: (519) 675-7631

LHIN: South West
Area: London
Phone Number: (519) 675-7631

LHIN: Waterloo Wellington
Area: Hamilton
Phone Number: (905) 546-8215

LHIN: Hamilton Niagara
Area: Hamilton
Phone Number: (905) 546-8215

LHIN: Mississauga Halton
Area: Hamilton
Phone Number: (905) 546-8215

LHIN: Central West
Area: Hamilton
Phone Number: (905) 546-8215

LHIN: Toronto Central
Area: Toronto
Phone Number: (416) 327-8984

LHIN: Central
Area: Toronto
Phone Number: (416) 327-8984

LHIN: Central East
Area: Ottawa

Phone Number: (613) 364-2269

LHIN: South East
Area: Ottawa
Phone Number: (613) 364-2269

LHIN: Champlain
Area: Ottawa
Phone Number: (613) 364-2269

LHIN: North Simcoe Muskoka
Area: Toronto
Phone Number: (416) 327-8984

LHIN: North East
Area: Sudbury
Phone Number: (705) 564-7489

LHIN: North West
Area: Sudbury
Phone Number: (705) 564-748

QUESTIONNAIRE

The following is a list of questions that will assist you in choosing a Long-Term Care home. Most deal with rights legislated in Bill 140, but the questions will clarify these rights for both you and the facility.

Upon your initial visit, you may find it helpful to take the questionnaire with you and also a list of your own questions to ask the administrator. Be sure to take notes of what you learn on your visit.

1. What is the application procedure?

2. What are the accommodation fee co-payments?

3. What services are included in the fees, e.g. personal supplies?

4. For what services is the resident/family responsible?

5. How and when are residents/families notified of a change in fees/services?

6. What is the facility's policy on restraints and medication?

7. What is the facility's policy on cardiopulmonary resuscitation? (It is not necessary to sign a DNR form on admission.)

8. Can you continue receiving care from your family doctor after admission to the facility?

9. Is the staff physician a geriatrician?

10. Is a physician on call 24 hours a day?

11. Are the physicians and/or medical director available to take calls from families?

12. Is the staff physician willing to spend time talking to family members regarding medical care of their family member?

13. Are special needs and preferences recognized by the facility? For example, do residents have a choice of showering or bathing? Do residents have the option of having breakfast in their robes?

14. If English is not the resident's first language, will an interpreter be available when necessary?

15. If applicable, are there programs and services available to meet the diverse cultural needs of the residents?

16. Inquire about residents' assessments and care plans:

    a) How often do case conferences occur?
    b) Are residents and representatives (substitute decision makers) involved in the case conferences and planning for the resident's care?
    c) Are the assessment information and care plans available to residents and family (or substitute decision makers)? How often are the care plan review meetings?

16. Is there free access to the facility? At what times? Are people, for example, volunteers, encouraged to visit?

17. Is there a volunteer program in the facility?

18. Are pastors, rabbis, and priests encouraged to visit?

19. Are married couples housed together?

20. Are physiotherapy, speech therapy, occupational therapy, bladder and bowel training available? Who arranges for these?

21. Are staff trained to work with the visually impaired and hearing impaired residents?

22. Are dentists and dental hygienists available to provide dental care? Who arranges for this?

23. Are community social work services available at the resident's request?

24. How many residents live in the facility?

25. How many floors are there?

26. How many elevators are there?

27. Are there regular fire drills for all staff (including part-time)?

28. Does the local fire inspector make regular visits?

29. Does the staff have training in managing difficult/aggressive behaviour?

30. Is there a government-approved smoking room?

You may have a list of your own questions to ask.

LONG-TERM CARE HOME CHECKLIST

Following your initial visit, review all the material given to you. Make arrangements for an informal visit. Before going for your second visit, review the Long-Term Care Home Checklist provided below.

Name of Facility:

Address:

Date of Visit:

Time:

Care of Residents

	YES	NO
1. Residents are clean (nails, hair, skin, teeth).	❑	❑

	YES	NO
2. Residents receive proper mouth care (breath smells fresh, mouth clean).	❑	❑
3. Residents are free from odour.	❑	❑
4. Residents are properly dressed.	❑	❑
a) Residents are wearing clothing which is clean and in good repair.	❑	❑
b) Residents' clothing fits and is done up.	❑	❑
c) Residents are wearing shoes and stockings which fit and match.	❑	❑

	YES	NO
5. Residents are wearing daytime apparel in the day, and night-time apparel at night.	❑	❑
6. Residents appear well groomed. (Men are shaved; residents have clean hair, cut and trimmed.)	❑	❑
7. Residents are dry and not soiled.	❑	❑
8. Residents seem to be properly fed (not too thin and frail).	❑	❑
9. Residents are receiving sufficient fluids at meal times and with all snacks.	❑	❑
10. Residents speak freely and openly with visitors. (They do not appear frightened or intimidated.)	❑	❑
11. Most residents are free from restraints. (Restraints include chairs with trays, bed sheets, and jacket restraints.)	❑	❑
12. Staff help residents change their positions in chairs or beds regularly. (Residents are not left slumped over or sliding from chairs.)	❑	❑
13. Residents are awake and not in bed midday.	❑	❑

	YES	NO
14. Residents appear alert.	❑	❑
15. Residents' eyes are clear; speech is not slurred. (Eyes are not blurry or "far away" which might signal over-medication.)	❑	❑
16. Residents are free from decubitus ulcers (bedsores).	❑	❑
17. Residents' feet, ankles, and legs are free from swelling and ulcerations; or, if swollen, are properly elevated.	❑	❑
18. Residents are free from evidence of injury (bruising, swelling, lacerations, stitches, casts, etc.).	❑	❑

Staff

	YES	NO
1. Sufficient staff are in evidence at nursing stations and on the floor.	❑	❑
2. Staff seem to be properly trained and address residents' needs in a caring and professional manner.	❑	❑
3. Staff smile, appear cheerful and show a caring attitude towards residents.	❑	❑

	YES	NO
4. Staff treat residents, family and other staff with courtesy, dignity and respect.	❑	❑
5. Staff are well groomed.	❑	❑
6. Staff are willing to answer questions and discuss needs of residents with family members.	❑	❑

General Surroundings

	YES	NO
1. Residents in wheelchairs are not lined up in the hallways or lounge areas.	❑	❑
2. The facility is totally accessible to wheelchairs (wide corridors and doors, ground-level access, specially designed bathrooms).	❑	❑
3. There are enough elevators. (Residents don't have to line up for a long time to go to and from the dining room.)	❑	❑
4. Floors and walls are clean, in good repair, and the decor is cheerful.	❑	❑
5. The home looks and smells clean.	❑	❑

	YES	NO
6. The home is free of evidence of cockroaches and rodents.	❑	❑
7. There are bright, pleasant lounge areas.	❑	❑
8. There is soft, pleasant music or activity in lounge areas.	❑	❑
9. Confused residents have safe areas in which to wander both inside and outside the home.	❑	❑
10. Residents have access to attractive outdoor surroundings with areas to sit or walk.	❑	❑
11. There are private areas for residents and visitors.	❑	❑
12. Other visitors are in evidence.	❑	❑
13. There is coffee, tea and juice available for residents and visitors.	❑	❑
14. Residents' rooms are bright and home-like, with personal belongings in evidence.	❑	❑
15. Residents can control heat and light in their bedrooms.	❑	❑

	YES	NO
16. Are there provisions for privacy for residents who share a room?	❏	❏
17. There is a call bell at each bed and within easy reach of resident.	❏	❏
18. There is an easy chair for every resident in each bedroom.	❏	❏
19. Closets in bedrooms are spacious and easily accessible to resident.	❏	❏
20. Can residents use a phone, cable television or a computer in their rooms?	❏	❏
21. There are a sufficient number of washrooms for residents.	❏	❏
22. Bathrooms are clean and odour free.	❏	❏
23. Bathing areas are clean and in good repair; tiles are not chipped.	❏	❏
24. There is sufficient clean linen and towels for residents' use.	❏	❏
25. Wheelchairs, trays and other equipment are clean and in good condition.	❏	❏

	YES	NO
26. The home has the Residents' Bill of Rights, Compliance Review Report, financial report, and Resident and Family Council information posted for public viewing in a conspicuous place.	❏	❏
27. Staff converse pleasantly with residents and visitors.	❏	❏
28. Residents' privacy is respected. (Staff knock before they enter and leave when visitors arrive. Privacy curtains are used appropriately and in good condition.)	❏	❏
29. Residents feel secure and do not appear to fear harm by staff or other residents, or theft of their belongings.	❏	❏
30. There is an active Residents' Council.	❏	❏
31. There is an active, independently run Family Council.	❏	❏

Rehabilitation/Restorative Care

	YES	NO
1. Age appropriate activity programs are in evidence (e.g. bridge games, poker, gardening, chess, woodworking, ceramics, painting, music, etc.).	❏	❏

	YES	NO
2. Individual orientation programs are in evidence for confused residents.	❏	❏
3. There are exercise programs for residents.	❏	❏
4. The majority of residents seem busy and occupied in a meaningful activity during the day.	❏	❏
5. There is a tuck shop.	❏	❏
6. The home has a library or visiting library service.	❏	❏
7 Organized activities are posted for month.	❏	❏

Dietary

	YES	NO
1. Snacks are served between meals and choices of beverages and snacks are available.	❏	❏
2. Meals appear appetizing and attractive.	❏	❏
3. Family members are welcome to join the resident at meal time.	❏	❏
4. There are culturally appropriate foods available.	❏	❏

	YES	NO
5. There are sufficient staff available to assist residents with eating when necessary.	❏	❏
6. Food meets any therapeutic needs residents may have (e.g. diabetic, salt free, chopped, pureed).	❏	❏
7. Food seems to be good nutritional value.	❏	❏
8. Fresh fruit and vegetables served, and there is adequate fibre.	❏	❏
9. Portions are large enough, and residents are offered second helpings.	❏	❏
10. Residents do not appear hungry and do not indicate that they are hungry or thirsty when asked.	❏	❏
11. Juices are served in 6-ounce glasses rather than 4-ounce glasses and water is offered between snacks.	❏	❏
12. Residents are encouraged to eat and drink.	❏	❏
13. Aides sit to assist residents with eating rather than standing over them.	❏	❏

	YES	NO	Scoring

14. Residents are fed individually, not in assembly-line fashion. ❑ ❑

To score this checklist, count one for every "yes" answer

15. Dietary staff respect residents' individual eating habits. That is, cleanup after meals is not rushed. ❑ ❑

71 to 80   very well operated facility

61 to 70   has reasonable amenities for residents

16. Residents are not segregated at meal time according to individual diets (e.g. puree, diabetic, etc.). ❑ ❑

below 61   facility should not be considered

Revised June 2007

17. Menus are displayed in clear view, on all floors and offer an alternative choice. ❑ ❑

18 Staff oversee residents as they eat, whether in dining room, own room or corridors. ❑ ❑

19. Dining room is attractive, pleasant and appropriately decorated. ❑ ❑

LEVELS OF CARE

Home Health Care

Home health care services — such as personal care, homemaking, nursing, or physiotherapy — may come from government-funded or private for-profit or not-for-profit firms. Community support services — such as friendly visiting or meals on wheels — may come from charitable and volunteer organizations. These networks of services aim to let seniors or younger handicapped individuals remain in their own homes and communities, living as independently as possible.

Retirement Residences

These are for people who can live independently but want to live among other seniors. These residences are designed and built to cater to the desires and lifestyles of seniors, offering accessible accommodations where mature individuals can feel safe yet remain active. Retirement residences are generally not subsidized. Non-profit retirement residences often offer subsidies for low-income seniors.

Long-Term Care Homes

Long-term care homes offer medical and personal support to seniors and younger handicapped individuals who need help around the clock. They are operated by private enterprise, local municipalities, or charitable organizations. Along the continuum of accommodations catering to seniors, long-term care homes (in the past often called nursing homes or homes for the aged) offer the most intensive level of supervision and medical services under one roof.

Who Is Eligible to Enter into a Long-Term Care Home

Individuals requiring twenty-four-hour nursing care and daily personal support services as well as seniors who are at risk in their own homes. Priority is based on need as assessed by the Community Care Access Centre, and the person must have a valid health card. Other people who are eligible are those who are unable to live independently in their own homes, even with an array of community services.

*The above information was summarized from *Comfort Life* magazine, 2005, a guide to retirement living and health care options.

LONG-TERM CARE AND SPIRITUALITY AND RELIGION

Ed Clements, Past Director of Pastoral Care, Christie Gardens

Incredible wisdom can be gleaned from the lifelong faith journeys of mature adults who live dynamic, fulfilling, and rich lives. It is from their heritage that we can inherit and learn valuable life lessons. Their spiritual lives are something of great value that needs to be expressed and shared. In any long-term care community, the need for spiritual care is essential. Everyone has some part of them that longs for transcendence, a rising above the mundane part of this world. We all look for commonality, a fitting in with those we are close to, whether that closeness comes from similar ideas or simply because we see ourselves reflected in the diverse community of which we are a part.

Faith is something that can join us together. It may be a lengthy faith journey or it may only come into focus as one nears the end of this life. Either way, its expression needs to be determined by the person being served. As a pastoral care director, I have seen people who have previously not been interested in faith discussions open up as they face the closing days of their lives. I have seen others walk gracefully out of this life, full of practical faith, ready to embrace the fulfillment of their hope in the next. It is a great privilege to have earned the right to be a listening ear, a kind heart, a confessor, an encourager, or a guide to deepen one's walk through life's end. No one should have to approach this important finality alone. It is where spirit and truth become one. It can provide peace that passes all human understanding.

At this critical juncture, serving both the resident as well as his or her loved ones allows for healthy closure. Even if there is no apparent need for closure expressed, once a person has died there is no turning back, no future opportunities to say that one thing they wished they had said. Providing a forum for a family to say goodbye and for all to finish well can have a lasting positive impact; even joy in a time of grief.

It is a privilege to serve in this way.

Irene Borins Ash

In the long, cold winter that I referred to in the introduction, the definition I came up with for the word *spirituality* during my research is as follows: "Spirituality has to do with issues of depth and significance in human life. Spirituality often involves asking ultimate questions. It is the way in which an individual creates a relationship with a larger, more inclusive dimension of being. Spirituality relates to questions of source, centre, meaning, and connection."

A friend described spirituality as a bridge between psychology and religion. Although organized religion addresses questions about the meaning and order of life, spirituality is seen as the way in which we find personal meaning in ourselves and our world.

Spirituality is something that each individual discovers for him or herself. It is often based on our own experience, not on following a given doctrine. Therefore the spiritual is not necessarily the religious. Religion is a bridge to the spiritual, but the spiritual lies beyond religion. True spirituality is based on personal experiences and is an extremely important and vital dimension of life. Spirituality nourishes, empowers, and gives meaning to human life.

I began to see that my love of music, gardening, and nature were my ways of connecting to the spiritual. These passions were the way in which I gave personal meaning to myself and the world around me. Also, my love of dogs was a big component of my spirituality. I cannot leave that out!

I have interviewed more than one hundred people between my first and my second book. I found that around 80 percent of the people I interviewed were religious or spiritual or both, and this helped them with the difficulties that life presents to everyone. Those that said religion and or spirituality did not help them in the difficult times said that their power and belief in themselves is what helped them.

Harry Lynch, Spiritual and Religious Care Manager, Providence Healthcare

For individuals, families, and caregivers, the decision to move to a long-term care home — although the most suitable option for many — is an extremely difficult one. The transition period can be challenging, but if handled with thoughtfulness and sensitivity it can open a new chapter in life for the residents and their families. After working at Providence Healthcare as a chaplain for more than twenty years, I have seen the hardship of having to let go and enter a new stage of one's life. The Cardinal Ambrozic Houses of Providence is the long-term care home at Providence Healthcare, and it offers home-like care for 288 residents. I have witnessed that this transition to long-term care can indeed be a time of entering into a new community of friends and supports. Because the individual's medical, physical, emotional, and spiritual needs are looked after in a supportive environment, their friends, their pastor or minister, and their "club buddies" can more easily connect with them in an accessible, elderly-friendly environment. It is a paradox that rather than being isolated in their house, the elderly resident now has the freedom, the dignity, and the independence to welcome friends and relatives.

Because of the environment of the Houses, the residents now have a chance to participate once again in their religious ritual of choice: daily Mass, Protestant service, or Anglican worship. These are activities that may have been disconnected through isolation, fear of slipping and falling, or transportation issues. Spiritual needs are significant and included in the care of every person within the Houses of Providence.

Within the community of the Houses of Providence we face seasons together and possibly open their spiritual lives to something new. One example is the Christmas Carolling and Tree-Lighting Ceremony, which brings the memories of Christmas alive for all who participate.

A new non-denominational service at the Houses has been developed to respond to the spiritual needs of residents with dementia. This worship service for the cognitively impaired has been developed for those residents who wish to participate but are unable to attend large group functions. We have found that a large group gathering for persons with dementia can be frightening and overstimulating. The residents are brought to a small, quiet room, apart from their activities of daily living. They are warmly welcomed and made to feel comfortable by familiar hymns and religious symbols. They are free to call out or sing and be accepted. This celebration creates that openness to wonderment, recapturing a lost sense of self in faith or a soft spiritual joy that we as a team in the Houses offer this person who has left their house.

A HISTORY OF A FAMILY-OWNED LONG-TERM CARE HOME: CRAIGLEE

BY CEILIA McDOUGALL, ASSISTANT ADMINISTRATOR

The journey begins March 15, 1958. What was to become a home to so many was created.

Craiglee Nursing Home at 102 Craiglee Drive began humbly as a thirteen-bed, 1800-square-foot house nestled in beautiful residential Cliffside, the perfect spot to be the future home to so many. The house had previously been owned by Mr. and Mrs. Ward and was a licensed and functioning long-term care residence before it was purchased by Roy and Doris McDougall. Doris was a registered nurse and dietician who trained in England after emigrating from Jamaica. Roy was the first black inspector Toronto Hydro ever had.

Duties were quickly distributed. Doris handled laundry, diets, and all aspects of nursing. Roy handled maintenance and all mechanical aspects of the operation. I barely remember the old house, but I *do* have clear memories of the residents who called Craiglee home at that time.

The McDougalls decided to expand. The petition proposed was for twenty-eight beds, which was granted. Roy continued to work at Toronto Hydro, and Doris went head-on into the successful operation of Craiglee Nursing Home.

Doris McDougall always maintained the essential combination of love, grace, compassion, and the ability to relate to others. Those in need always found assistance at Craiglee. Her British nursing training is ever present in her operation of the home and in her expectations of her staff: to always take the best possible care of the residents and to treat them as they would want their own family treated. She never settles for second best and is always a solid advocate for the residents entrusted to her care.

The 1970s and 1980s brought two more expansions, bringing the number of beds to ninety-four. The latest expansion was completed in the spring of 2004, and we now have 169 beds in an 80,000-square-foot home.

I am proud to have learned about long-term care from such dedicated and committed individuals; they are truly trendsetters in long-term care. The legacy of Craiglee Nursing Home is still as strong in the community. We continue to take pride in the utmost quality of care.

LISTENING TO THE RESIDENTS

BY GILBERT HEFFERN
DIRECTOR OF COMMUNICATIONS AND PUBLIC AFFAIRS, OLTCA

The following letter, sent to the editor of the *Toronto Star* and copied to the Ontario Long Term Care Association, speaks to a weakness in the media and public policy debates on long-term care. The letter was written in 2008 in response to media stories generated by a Canadian Press review of long-term care compliance data collected by Ontario's Ministry of Health and Long-Term Care and published on the ministry's Reports on Long-Term Care Homes website (www.health.gov.on.ca/english/public/program/ltc/26_reporting.html).

We are, respectively, the President and Executive Director of the Ontario Association of Residents' Councils, a 26-year-old association of Residents' Councils in Ontario's long-term care homes. All of our Board, including our President, are residents of long-term care homes across the province. As such, they are the best witnesses to what their homes are like and what they mean to them. Yet, no one asks them what things they like about their homes, what makes them proud of their own home and happy to call it home.

Your newspaper and others, including Canadian Press in its study of compliance/inspection reports, have zeroed in on the few bad apples in the very large "bushel" of 620-plus homes, leaving readers to believe that things are in very bad shape, and that readers and prospective residents should be in a state of alarm, even fear, about the prospect of life in a long-term care home. That is simply not the case, and we would like to tell you that at our recent Board meetings, members (residents) spent two hours discussing their views on what things should be like in Ontario's homes. They repeatedly referred to all the good things that are going on in so many homes and how proud they were of their own homes.

Yes, they saw things that could be improved, or changed, but tellingly they spoke more often of what they liked, the myths that others may hold, and why they were generally very pleased with their homes and eager to tell others so. On their behalf and our thousands of members across Ontario, we are urging you and your readers to listen to the voices of actual residents. Why not consider visiting a long-term care home to talk to and listen to residents? They are the best witnesses, and they know that so many good homes, and so many good things, are being ignored. What you would hear would provide you with a more balanced and fair story of life in a long term care home. Try it.

Maureen Hutchinson, President
Pat Prentice, Executive Director
Ontario Association of
Residents' Councils

Ms. Hutchinson and Ms. Prentice make a poignant plea based on a valid point. The collective voice of those best positioned to comment credibly on the state of long-term care is most often the voice that is missing from the media and public policy debates. Instead, what one often gets is a single resident voice that stands as a reflection of the collective, or third-party statements that serve as a proxy voice.

In the case of Ontario, that would be a single or third-party voice attempting to reflect almost seventy-six thousand voices. It is not surprising that it often appears to have an overriding paternalistic flavour.

In the case of the media, the nature of news is such that this voice will seldom, if ever, be complimentary. In fact, the reflection of a differing opinion is often relegated to the letters section or, more recently, the Web site commentary section. While letters and Web site commentaries are valued spaces for discussion and debate, they do not have the same prominence as the front page of your morning newspaper or the lead story on the evening news.

Ms. Hutchinson and Ms. Prentice make a strong case for an increased level of media diligence in reporting long-term care stories. In fact, their message should provide food for thought for any one when addressing the subject of long-term care.

The absence of a collective or strong resident voice from media and public policy discussions on long-term care has been recognized as a weakness by those who work in or provide service to the sector. At the same time, it has to be recognized that the sector itself does not make it easy or efficient for members of the media or others to practice this higher level of diligence.

For example, there is no publicly accessible record of how residents or their families collectively feel about the quality and value of the care and services provided by either the sector as a whole or by an individual home. Homes receive lots of cards and letters that express appreciation for their care and services they provide. Sometimes these make it into the local community newspaper, get posted inside the home, or otherwise move into the public domain. For the most part, however, it would appear that these tributes remain within the internal operating parameters of the individual homes.

Similarly, most homes do have some form of satisfaction surveying that gives residents and families a voice. The results of these surveys, however, are generally considered internal to the home — even if they are shared, to some degree, with Residents' Councils or other groups. Even if the results of these surveys were made public, the media would not likely find such internally driven initiatives to be a credible source of information, regardless of whether the results were derived from a home-grown survey tool or one administered by a third-party service provider.

In short, widespread access to the sources and stories that represent the collective full-spectrum voice of residents is in short supply. It would be a mistake to assume that increasing this supply would challenge every media story or third-party assessment. Most likely it would be a mixed bag. It would, however, allow those to whom such conclusions and judgments matter the most to have a stronger say in the process and thus inject a higher degree of confidence into the outcome.

In this book Ms. Borins Ash begins to take an important step forward to address this deficiency. In photographing the subjects for her *Aging Is Living* photo exhibit she took the time to listen to and record their stories. The result is a not often seen image of long-term care residents and of long-term care through their eyes. It is an image that challenges many of the myths and stereotypes of not only long-term care but also aging itself.

It demonstrates that all of us need to hear more from the voice that is too often missing now.

The foregoing has been adapted from an original column by Gilbert Heffern that appeared in the September/October 2008 edition of Long Term Care *magazine (www.oltca.com).*

TIPS FOR PLANNING AS A PERSON AGES

BY IRENE BORINS ASH

One of the first pieces of advice I can offer is that of prevention. Do everything that you can do to stay healthy for as long as possible. In my first book, *Treasured Legacies: Older & Still Great*, Hazel McCallion, mayor of Mississauga since 1978, was interviewed; at age eighty-seven she was and even now still is energetic, passionate, and a role model for everyone. Mayor McCallion believes that we must take responsibility for our own health. She stated that she "strongly believes that people should empower themselves by being as self-reliant as possible and take responsibility for their mental and physical health." People need to focus on what they can do, not on what they cannot do.

Also in *Treasured Legacies*, Dr. Bernard Ludwig stated, "I believe that aging begins at conception and continues throughout life. The earlier we become aware of our aging process, the better we will fare in our later years. Discipline is a key factor: overeating, lack of exercise, smoking, and excess alcohol all hinder our ability to age well. Exercising on a regular basis and eating correctly and monitoring our intake can slow down the aging process. Although genetics play an important part in the process, habits of self-discipline can overshadow heredity."

I will also add that being conservative with prescription medication is important for positive and healthy aging. Over-medication is a major problem with seniors, and at times the medications interact poorly with each other. Try to find a doctor who is conservative and cautious about prescribing medication.

Making decisions about the later part of one's life is not easy, but it is important that everyone knows that there are many options available as we grow older.

Many services are provided to help seniors live in their own homes safely, as so many people want to remain active and independent for as long as possible.

Although I am making specific references to Ontario organizations in these tips, there are similar programs in other Canadian provinces as well in the United States.

Keeping seniors healthy and independent as long as possible by proper geriatric assessment and treatment can save the system millions of dollars each year. There are numerous older adult centres that provide activities and socialization for seniors who are living in their own homes. In my introduction, I talked about St. Clair West Services for Seniors as I was a case manager in that organization, but there are numerous similar centres all over the province and the country. The centres' activities and programs help the seniors' physical, mental, and emotional well-being. There are exercise programs, outings, lectures, computer classes, gardening programs, pet therapy programs, and many more. There are also associations such as the Older Adult Centres' Association of Ontario (OACAO) and the Ontario Community Support Association (OCSA).

Two other interesting organizations are the Older Women's Network (OWN) and the Performance Arts Lodge (PAL). OWN strives to achieve a caring society in which older and mid-life women have the opportunity to live in security and with dignity; to participate in the choices affecting their lives; to give mutual support and share interests and activities; and to realize their potential. OWN is a voice in our changing, diverse Canadian society that challenges discrimination on the basis of age, gender, sexual orientation, race, ethnic origin, religion, or disability. PAL is a community-based retirement home in Toronto and other locations in Canada that provides affordable housing and improved living conditions for those in the performing arts professions. By living in a residence like PAL, the resident is less isolated and they

have the support of others from a similar profession. They are living in a vibrant community. Some residents have disabilities and are nearing the end of their lives.

If you have been in a hospital you will probably have met with a discharge planner who will help you decide what the next step will be. Once you are ready to return to the community the discharge planner guides and supports the patient and the family through the various options that are available. When the patient is discharged from the hospital the local Community Care Access Centre (CCAC) will help organize home care or long-term care if necessary.

Staying at home may be better for some but not for everyone, and much depends on resources and support from family and/or community. The Ontario Homecare Association (OHCA) represents home health care organizations that provide home care services throughout rural and urban Ontario. The OHCA is a leader in promoting provision of adequate financial and other resources for the home and community care sector in Ontario. The association participates regularly, both federally and provincially, in task forces, consultations, and committees in order to develop consistent approaches to policy and funding issues affecting home and community care service provision. Home support agencies provide services such as nursing, physiotherapy, nutrition counselling, occupational therapy, personal support, housekeeping, transportation, palliative care, and in-home diagnostic and lab procedures and dialysis.

The most important tip I can offer is to plan as much as possible in advance and to educate yourself. If you are looking for a bed in a long-term care home there may be a long waiting list, so if you want your place of choice plan in advance. It is best when seniors works with their children on the planning where this is possible, but even if there are no adult children involved it still takes time to find out what is wanted and go on the waiting list if necessary. Finding a doctor who has specific geriatric training is wise.

It is also important to plan financially, if possible, for your old age. When you are checking out possible retirement homes or long-term care homes make sure you educate yourself on all of the financial factors.

When choosing a retirement residence or long-term care home, it is important to be in a familiar location and close to family and friends. If you want to learn more about retirement residences in Ontario you can refer to the Ontario Retirement Communities Association at 1-800-361-7254. Retirement residences interest men and women who can live independently, but want to live with other seniors. Retirement residences provide variations of design and services that meet the lifestyle of the seniors and they provide services that enable to senior to be active yet feel safe.

When more care is necessary, a long-term care home can be a better option. Long-term care homes offer medical and personal support to seniors who need care twenty four hours a day. They are operated by private enterprise, local municipalities or charitable

organizations and offer the most intensive level of supervision and medical care in one facility.

There are two organizations that represent long-term care homes: the Ontario Long Term Care Association (OLTCA) and the Ontario Association of Non-Profit Homes and Services for Seniors (OANHSS). OLTCA is the largest long-term care providers' organization in Ontario, representing the private, not-for-profit, charitable, and municipal operators of approximately 430 of the almost 600 long-term care homes in the province that provide care and services to 50,000 residents. OANHSS represents long-term care homes as well as seniors' housing and community agencies that provide care and services on a not-for-profit basis only.

Regarding Ontario government legislation and monitoring of long-term care homes, the Ministry of Health and Long-Term Care sets the standards for care and inspects long-term care homes annually. It also sets the rules governing eligibility and waiting lists. All homes must post and follow a Residents' Bill of Rights. The ministry is continually working on providing the best care for their residents and on trying to improve the quality of life, which can be variable, in long-term care homes. As this book shows, there are many people leading quality lives in long-term care.

LIST OF LONG-TERM CARE HOMES THAT
SUBJECTS ARE RESIDENT IN

Nikola Vasic
Home: Leisureworld Caregiving Centre — O'Connor
Court, Toronto, Ontario

Ronald Ponsford
Home: Wellesley Central Place, Toronto, Ontario

Norval E. Tooke
Home: Kensington Health Centre, Toronto, Ontario

Eleanor G. Munro
Home: Kensington Health Centre, Toronto, Ontario

Elizabeth Rodrigo
Personal Support Worker

Irene Greenbloom
Home: Baycrest Centre for Geriatric Care, Toronto,
Ontario

Mae Merkley (née Contois)
Home: Hillcrest Village Care Centre, Midland, Ontario

David Chadwick
Sylvia Chadwick (née Sone)
Home: Extendicare Bayview, Toronto, Ontario

Evelyn Rosemund Williams
Home: Rekai Centre, Toronto, Ontario

Zev Selinger
Home: Lincoln Place Long Term Care Home, Toronto,
Ontario

Earl Edial Joseph Albrecht
Home: Leisureworld Caregiving Centre — Ellesmere,
Scarborough, Ontario

Robert (Bob) E. Ransom
Josephine (Beth) Ransom
Home: The Westbury, Etobicoke, Ontario

Andrew Roberts
Home: Bethany Lodge, Unionville, Ontario

Maureen Hutchinson
Home: West Park Long Term Care Centre, Toronto,
Ontario

Edward (Eddie) Siman
Home: The Village of Erin Meadows, Mississauga,
Ontario

Vernon McCutcheon
Home: Specialty Care Bradford Valley, Bradford,
Ontario

Eleanor M. (Ellis) Russell
Home: Specialty Care Mississauga Road, Mississauga,
Ontario

Philip O. McHale
Home: Garden Terrace, Nepean, Ontario

Colleen Taffe
Home: Cardinal Ambrozic Houses of Providence, Scarborough, Ontario

Ruth Adams
Home: Extendicare Oshawa, Oshawa, Ontario

Bruce E. Hutcheson
Home: Christie Gardens, Toronto, Ontario

Helen Niles
Home: Extendicare Lakefield, Lakefield, Ontario

Luong Vien
Home: O'Neill Centre, Toronto, Ontario

Alan Philp
Home: Community Nursing Home, Pickering, Ontario

Sharon Dyer
Home: Craiglee Nursing Home, Scarborough, Ontario

Natalie Guzik
Home: Stirling Heights Long Term Care Centre,
Cambridge, Ontario

Irene Borins Ash

Irene Borins Ash is a social worker, speaker, and photographer whose focus is on helping people of all ages, particularly seniors, develop a positive attitude towards aging despite life's difficulties. She is a Registered Social Worker with a Master of Social Work, and has been on staff at several health care facilities and presented papers across the country.

Irene is a passionate photographer who uses the camera to tell stories and capture the inner essence of the person. She loves to walk on the beach in Toronto, spend time with her nieces and nephews, ride her bike, visit dogs, listen to a wide variety of music, travel, and go to movies with her husband, Irv.

Irv Ash

Irv Ash is a native-born Torontonian but was a lawyer in a Calgary law firm in the 1980s for six years. Returning to Toronto after a round-the-world trip, he was a corporate executive for seven years with various companies, including being a vice-president at Cineplex Odeon Corporation. He then decided that his real profession was teaching, and after nine years part-time teaching at various Toronto colleges he has been a full-time professor at Seneca College since 2001. Happily married to Irene Borins Ash since 2000, he has also written various works, assisted Irene in her work, played tennis, downhill skied, and watched numerous movies. He has personally experienced long-term care while assisting his mother, Nellie, during the last three years of her life.

MARQUIS

Marquis Book Printing Inc.

Québec, Canada

2009